Clarity
— to —

MAKE YOUR MARK

12 steps to discovering your vision,
being your best self, and leaving a legacy

Jessica Ritchie

First published 2022 by Jessica Ritchie

Produced by Indie Experts P/L, Australasia
indieexperts.com.au

Text and illustrations copyright © Jessica Ritchie 2022

The moral right of the author to be identified as the author of this work has been asserted.

Apart from any fair dealing for the purposes of study, research or review, as permitted under the copyright act, no part of this book may be reproduced by any process without written permission of the author.

Every effort has been made to trace and acknowledge copyright material; should any infringement have occurred accidentally, the author tends her apologies.

Product and other names used herein may be trademarks of their respective owners. The author disclaims any and all rights in those marks.

Cover design by Daniela Catucci @ Catucci Design
Edited by Anne-Marie Tripp
Internal design by Indie Experts
Typeset in 10.75/16 pt Abril Text by Post Pre-press Group, Brisbane

ISBN 978-0-6453836-0-7 (paperback)
ISBN 978-0-6453836-2-1 (hardback)
ISBN 978-0-6453836-1-4 (epub)

Disclaimer: Every effort has been made to ensure this book is as accurate and complete as possible. However, there may be mistakes both typographical and in content. Therefore, this book should be used as a general guide and not and the ultimate source of information contained herein. The author and publisher shall not be liable or responsible to any person or entity with respect to any loss or damage caused or alleged to have been caused directly or indirectly by the information contained in this book.

For Daniel, for giving me the final nudge.

For those who want clarity to discover, or rediscover, their magic, pave their own paths, and leave a legacy. It's time to Make Your Mark.

Contents

Introduction to the "Your Mark" Series	xi
The "Your Mark" Series	xvii
To "Make Your Mark"	xxiv
Introduction to Book 1: Make Your Mark	1
Step 1: Identity & Sense of Self	9
Step 2: Self-Worth – Know Your Worth	35
Step 3: Vision – Permission to Dream	49
Step 4: Unwrap Your Unique Gifts	73
Step 5: Unshackle Your Fears	87
Step 6: Beliefs and Belief	103
Step 7: Turn Imposter into a Composer	119
Step 8: Comparisonitis – Do You Dare to Compare?	133
Step 9: Values – Your Guiding Lights	145
Step 10: Intuition – Finding Your Inner Guru	169
Step 11: Integrity – Even When Eyes Can't See	189
Step 12: Congruence Can Influence	203
Final Thoughts	217

Jessica Wants to Hear from You!	220
Acknowledgements	222
About Jessica Ritchie	225
Coming Soon in the "Your Mark" Series	227
About Jana Stanfield, CSP	231

Dear reader,

As a special bonus, I have created a swag of **FREE goodies** to help supercharge your journey to becoming a Make Your Mark Maestro!

Gain *exclusive* access to the **Make Your Mark Workbook** as a further resource to embed your learning from this book. You will also receive downloadable Make Your Mark Mantras, Personal Power Anthem Cards and the Make Your Mark Mastery Indicator.

To download your **free gifts**, go to https://jessica-ritchie.com/books/resources.

Here's to you Making Your Mark,

Introduction to the "Your Mark" Series

The motivation for me to write the "Your Mark" series was two-fold – the interweaving of threads from my personal and professional experience.

Personal Experience

Life throws us challenges. Challenges come in all different shapes and sizes. Some are like pebbles, minor irritations that barely leave a mark; others have the impact of a rock, painful and might leave a bruise for a while; and some are boulders that take you to your knees and all but wipe you out. Like many people, I've had a lot of challenges throughout my life, however there were four significant experiences that occurred to me over a six-year period. These experiences made me sit up and take notice of my existence and how I was living my life. (I talk about some of these experiences in more detail in this series, especially in *Make Your Mark*.)

At the beginning of 2011, I lost my home and all my possessions in the catastrophic Queensland floods. When I lost everything, all that was left, in a way, was ME – even though I felt like a shell of my former self. While I was rebuilding my home, I realised that I actually had to learn how to rebuild myself as well. I started to lay the foundations of building my new self. Later the same year, one of my dearest friends, Naomi, was diagnosed with stage four ovarian cancer. I was devastated. We were only twenty-five years old. At one of my last visits to Naomi in hospital, she said, out of the blue, "You know what, Jess? I've come to realise that before I had cancer, there were some aspects that I didn't like about myself, but since having cancer, I've made changes and I can now say I love who I am and who I've become."

It dawned on me that often it can take these monumental, life challenges for us to create change to become our best selves, and we can show ourselves compassion and kindness in the process. This is one of the lessons that made a mark on me in that moment.

Two years later, my brother Nathan was paralysed in an accident that happened on Easter Sunday. Receiving this news hit me (and my family) like a tonne of bricks. It certainly wasn't the phone call that I was expecting to receive first thing on Easter morning; I thought it was my nieces calling to say that the Easter Bunny had visited. How wrong I was. It was a very difficult time: feeling helpless, wishing that I could make my brother able to walk again, and remove the pain everyone was feeling. One silver lining was the quality time that I got to spend with Nathan, my sister-in-law Samantha, and my two gorgeous nieces, Maddison and Charlotte. They spent twelve months living only a few doors down from my house while my brother had intensive rehabilitation and care in a nearby hospital. I also witnessed the generosity and kindness of strangers delivering activity packs for the kids and meals for the family. Even though it was under difficult circumstances, I treasured every moment, felt so much gratitude that Nath survived, and became much more present and mindful with how I lived.

2017 brought a boulder experience that really propelled me to take action to create personal and professional change. Plastered across the national news headlines was a dire situation, still unfolding – a police officer had been shot and killed in the line of duty. With how the news media communicated the incident, for forty minutes I believed that that policeman was my husband, Sam. For those forty minutes, I was flipping from panic and sheer terror to deep reflection. I thought I'd lost my husband and it was the scariest, most painful moment in my life. But I also thought about how proud I was of Sam and the mark that he makes in the world each and every day. How he shows up, so present in his career and life. How I hadn't been doing the same. I realised how much I'd personally been holding back because of fear – mainly of what people would think or say, or how they would judge me … if I actually chose to create the life and the business I wanted. I was no longer scared of much at all having been through that experience. I vowed and declared that I was never going to live small again. That I would invest in myself and revisit the work that I started back in 2011 to rebuild myself stronger and more able than ever before.

I don't share these moments for sympathy. I know these are a drop in the ocean compared to what others have been through, **yet that's just it** – you cannot discount your experience by comparing your experience to those of others. Yes, it puts things into perspective. Yes, it may give you immense gratitude. However, as a friend of mine said, "but by theirs being 'worse', it doesn't make your experience any less."

I share just some of my experiences to say that I see you and that no matter how big or small we perceive a curveball to be, to hope that in some small way that how I overcame mine might inspire you. These moments leave a mark on us. It is up to us to allow life's challenges to change us, but not to become bitter; to become better. It is up to us how we can use them to shape us into more resilient human beings.

Each experience made me think, *Who am I? Who do I want to be? What regrets would I have if this was my last day on earth? Have I given it my all, my very best?* **Have I made my mark?**

Professional Experience

Now I also mentioned that I had professional experiences which motivated me to write the "Your Mark" series. For over fifteen years I've had the privilege of working with some of

Australia's leading and most recognised personal and business brands. Every day I get asked to create transformational people and brands through beautiful branding, kick-ass marketing strategies and communication plans. I love it. However, what I have found over the years is that even with the best branding and marketing strategy in place, it is OURSELVES that get in our own way and hold us back from going after what we want in business, career and life. I have seen some of the most sensational brands come undone because they don't have a strong foundation of **m**indset, **a**uthenticity, **r**esilience and **k**indness (MARK) on which to build their personal or business brand. According to the Australian Bureau of Statistics, more than 60% of small businesses fail within their first three years of starting,[1] and this doesn't surprise me when I think about how many people I have worked with who lacked that strong foundation.

I believe to get the best start possible, the first work that you need to do when going into business is on yourself. That is why, when I start working with clients, I rewind a few steps and go back to the foundational groundwork to uncover and rediscover who my clients are through life's trials and tribulations – because, let's face it, most of us don't take a lot of time to reflect when they happen and just keep powering on. I discover what it is that they truly stand for personally *and* professionally, their values, mission, their why – everything

---

[1] Libby-Jane Charleston, "Why Small Businesses Fail in Australia," *HuffPost*, September 27, 2015, https://www.huffpost.com/archive/au/entry/small-business-failure_n_8187166.

that is within *Make Your Mark,* the first book of this series. It's not about providing a great marketing strategy or logo and then hoping for the best. Having clarity and vision in place allows people and businesses to make their mark time and time again. And they can do it with confidence, and with impact in both big and little ways. Two-thirds of the work that I do with clients is working on the internal – their foundation, and their connection (explored in the second book of the series, *Spark Your Mark*) before we can ignite the external work, what the world sees (explored in the final book, *Ignite Your Mark*). The process is a bit like growing bamboo. When bamboo is planted with the right conditions, it can grow over ninety centimetres in just twenty-four hours! And I am assuming that this is what you want – to grow rapidly and confidently in the right conditions. The right foundation and conditions build sustainable holistic brands that make a mark.

In my work and throughout the "Your Mark" series, I also integrate tools and techniques that make me a bit different to other marketing and brand experts. My other skillsets of reiki master healing, neurolinguistic programming, business coaching and life coaching help embed, elevate and amplify my clients' journey. I use the exact same tools and techniques that I personally discovered through my own experiences to build brave brands, people and businesses that stand the test of time. The path of self-discovery and learning how to strengthen my mindset, be more authentic, resilient, and kinder is now what I teach others to do, too.

The "Your Mark" Series

There are three stages in **making your ultimate mark** in your business, career, and life. To make your ultimate mark, you need three Fs: your foundation, a fire and your fuel.

Well, actually maybe there are four Fs. You really do need to give a bit of a f*ck too, don't you reckon? It's very trendy these days to **not** give a f*ck, but you need to give a f*ck about yourself and about the legacy you're going to leave on the world so that you have the drive to move forward and Make Your Mark. I'm guessing that you have this first F already sorted– you give a f*ck, which is what drew YOU to this book. Now it is time to build upon the other three Fs.

Jessica Ritchie ©

Each book in the "Your Mark" series covers one of the Fs, and each book builds upon the last. Together, the three books show you how to build consistent, unshakeable, sustainable momentum to continually Make Your Mark – in both big and small ways. By the end of the series, you will have gained clarity and connection to communicate with confidence.

Book 1: MAKE Your Mark®

You need to create a solid foundation in order to Make Your Mark, just like a fire starts with a solid foundation of kindling. In this book, you'll discover how to build your foundation by getting **clarity and vision** around who you are and where you are going, through establishing a strong sense of self, self-worth, and uniqueness; clarifying your values, removing limiting beliefs, and unshackling fear; calling out imposter syndrome and "comparisonitis", following your intuition, maintaining integrity and being congruent in all that you do.

Book 2: SPARK Your Mark®

To create a spark, you need to **connect** with something, and in this book, we focus on the connection to yourself. You need connection to yourself first and foremost in order to truly connect with others. It's being your most authentic self, prioritising self-care, having a support tribe around you, knowing your boundaries, and – a super important point – increasing your **energy and vibration.** This is like the first spark of fire that you set to your foundation of kindling.

Book 3: IGNITE Your Mark®

Adding fuel to a spark on a good base of kindling makes a roaring, powerful fire. Adding fuel to your spark ignites your power on the inside, but also gives you a way to showcase it to the world on the outside. Your fire, your glow, is in how you **communicate** and increase your **visibility.** Fire is hard to ignore, it can be hot and fast, but instead of this fire being destructive, it will be your ultimate force in business, career and life – in igniting your mark. Communication is the fuel source for all that you do through your story, your personal brand elevation, your presence and presentation. This is what is required to leave your legacy and to continue to keep making your mark.

THE "YOUR MARK" MODEL

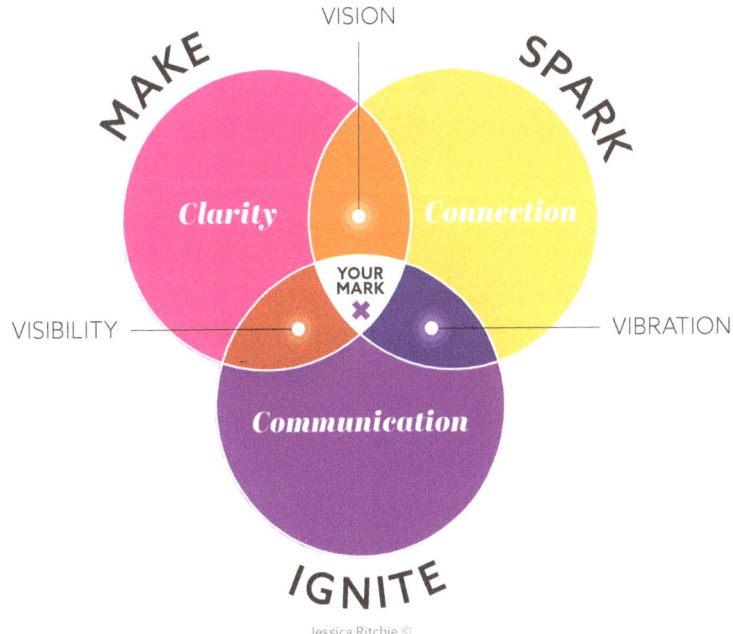

The three books of the "Your Mark" series work together to help you make your ultimate mark. There are three essential areas of self-development that are required to create your mark, personally and professionally.

At the intersection of clarity and connection is vision. This is where you reflect and focus on "the big picture" as you step up and take charge of the director's chair of your life. Your vision allows you to shine with confidence as you get clear on the strategy required to get to the next level to Make Your Mark. Enhanced intuition and clarity in your vision allows you to deeply connect to yourself and others so that you create your own power anthem and march to the beat of your own drum to accomplish your goals and become your best self in business, career and life.

At the intersection of connection and communication is vibration. Your energy is what sets you apart from others. Learn how to cultivate and harness your energy to your advantage through instinct, and learn how to release negative energy and protect yourself energetically from others. Your energetic elevation occurs through a strong connection to yourself where your high vibe will attract the right opportunities, people and support to get you to where you want to be.

At the intersection of communication and clarity is visibility. Communicating with a clear and consistent messaging that is authentic to you with your unique energy and essence will ignite your visibility to the world. Step into your personal power knowing that you are creating a positive impact and leaving a legacy both personally and professionally. You now have the key elements to Make Your Mark in your business, career and in life. When all three elements are brought together and are working in harmony, you will be in a position to Make Your Mark, with a foundation of mindset, authenticity, resilience and kindness in all that you do.

Harnessing the Power of MARK

Everything you need for the life you've been dreaming of is already inside you. You just need the right foundation to build upon in order to harness your unique potential and turn your vision into a reality.

To make, spark and ignite your mark in your business, career, and life, you need to harness the power within the word MARK.

Over the "Your Mark" series and within each book, we will zero in on four key areas to explode your growth:

M – Mindset. Adopting a positive mindset, knowing your self-worth and removing limiting beliefs. Not allowing imposter syndrome and comparing yourself to others stop you from achieving your goals and vision.

A – Authenticity. Having a strong sense of self. Knowing who you are, your identity, the essence of you, the energy that you exude. Living your values and vision unapologetically and congruently with the ability to communicate your story and radiate your essence to those in your presence.

R – Resilience. Remove any residue that weighs you down and dig deep into your reserves of strength, courage, bravery, and agility. Even if you've had a bad day and feel like you're a bit over it all, you open the door for a stranger, or you smile at the elderly lady walking towards you. You know that tomorrow is a new day and that there is no such thing as failure, just lessons to be learnt, and that resilience is a key to success.

K – Kindness. It is the kindling that can support the most amazing, positive sparks. Being kind to yourself (first and foremost) through self-compassion and self-care and keeping yourself as a priority is one of the biggest ways that you can Make Your Mark. This then allows you to pour from your cup, giving to others and integrating acts of kindness into your day. Doesn't the world need a little more kindness right about … now?

Developing these four elements will help you make your ultimate mark in your business, career and life. While all four of these elements underpin the theories explored in the "Your Mark" series, each book focuses on certain elements and how they integrate together. The first book, *Make Your Mark*, focuses on mindset and authenticity, resulting in increased resilience. The second book, *Spark Your Mark*, highlights the power of authenticity and kindness, particularly in connections and kindness with yourself. The third book, *Ignite Your Mark*, explores how you can communicate authenticity, resilience and kindness, while revisiting the concept of mindset – ensuring you have the tools and confidence to go forward and make your ultimate mark.

You can harness the power of your MARK, and live the life you deserve with no regrets.

To "Make Your Mark"

> *"If you're going to live, leave a legacy. Make a mark on the world that can't be erased."*
> — MAYA ANGELOU

Many people in life want to make their mark. But what does that mean?

For some, to Make Your Mark means to have your name in bright flashing lights, to be famous, for people to know of you and to be what society deems "successful". But making your mark is a deeply personal and varied thing: it doesn't necessarily mean that you need to become the CEO of the business that you're working for, or the most famous person in your field. It doesn't have to be big, bold and loud, where everyone knows who you are.

Making your mark is legacy creation, magic making, and no-regret living. It's getting the most out of this one wild and innately unique life you've been gifted. For me, those who want to make a mark have an internal drive – an internal spark that propels them forward in life and gives them the ability to keep digging deep, to continue to self-improve, to leave the world a better place, and to leave a legacy.

Making your mark is leaving your footprints behind on the paths that you will pave. A footprint leaves a mark on the surfaces it touches, and is entirely unique to you – just like your fingerprint. You can leave your footprints in the sand and at each and every change of tide, the waves inevitably wash your footprint away. There's no mark or indication that you were ever there. Instead of a loose, temporary foundation like sand, you can make the decision to leave your footprint in concrete, solidly embedded, a clear and consistent imprint that can survive all elements, will continue to make an impact long after you've gone, and marks out a path for others to follow.

To be honest with you, there have been many times I wish I didn't have the drive that keeps pushing me to make my mark. Why? Because it can feel like it makes life HARD! I talk about "Make Your Mark Moments" often throughout this series, sharing insights into what I've learnt or observed in others, and many times those learnings are the silver linings of what were really hard experiences. Making your mark takes a strong mindset, authenticity, resilience, commitment, kindness, energy, and an unwavering vision and belief in yourself. It's not for the faint hearted. It's not the easy road. It's the path less travelled, but the path you feel that you need to take. It might feel hard at times but hardly anyone has achieved greatness by taking the easy route.

> *"Either you make a mark on the world, or the world will make a mark on you."*
> — PAULO COELHO

There are tell-tale feelings that you might have when you feel like you are **not** making your mark. You might feel overwhelmed, frustrated, restless, uneasy, uncertain, or annoyed. You might have a sense that you can achieve your wildest dreams, to do more and be more, but you don't know how or where to start. You might be thinking, *What is my purpose in life? Why am I here? What have I been placed on this planet to achieve?*

You. Want. More. From. Life. You bear witness to other people going out and grabbing their dreams with both hands, yet something holds you back. How can they grab life with both hands when you're not sure you even have a finger grasp? You might feel stuck, even pissed off at times. You're not sure where to start. What you do know is that you just want to feel like you're on track, on purpose, and working towards a higher vision of being your best, most authentic self; to find some joy and flow in what you do.

Some days you will feel like you have made your mark and other times, you may not feel like you've done anything that is particularly special at all. It's like a road that feels like a rollercoaster – you're up, you're down, you're on your way, and whoah, hold on … now you're going backwards. *How do other people just cruise on through life?* you might be thinking. They don't, generally. Although I must admit sometimes there may be a lucky few. Setbacks and challenges are all part of the journey, part of the story that you're writing along the way. Making your mark isn't all about social greatness, **it is about establishing your personal greatness.**

By being here, you are on purpose. I know that sounds counterintuitive; you might be thinking, *Um, Jess, how can that be so, because I don't feel like I am doing anything super important or of immense value right now? I'm not making my mark by just waking up.*

Yes, you are. As humans, we place so much emphasis on tangible results and pressure on ourselves to perform. To find meaning. To be of value. For instant reward and recognition. But what I want to encourage you to think about is, maybe you did Make Your Mark or you do Make Your Mark without even realising it. How might you do that, you ask? You can (and do) Make Your Mark each and every day through moments. They are what I like to call Make Your Mark Moments. These moments can be as simple as smiling at a stranger, opening the café door for a mother who has her arms full, asking the grocery attendant how their day is going, checking in on a friend who is going through a hard time, "paying it forward" by buying a coffee for a stranger, cooking a meal for someone who is in need, or giving one hour of your time to a local charity. It could be like when my friend Naomi in all her vulnerability admitted that she now loved who she was because of cancer; one of the moments that inspired me to be a better person. My brother made his mark by inspiring me to never give up, the flood left its mark on me by giving me the push that I needed to find myself, and my husband's work incident was the catalyst for me to become my most authentic self in business and live to my full potential. Moments – little or big ones, positive or sad or scary ones – can leave a positive impact on you and those around you. These moments create a ripple effect that leave the world just that little bit better. I can guarantee you that you are already making your mark for those around you, but it's also important to learn how you can Make Your Mark in bolder, stronger, more intentional ways. With a strong identity and vision to Make Your Mark, you get to leave your mark in the world more strongly than the marks the world might leave on you.

Why Does Making Your Mark Matter?

To Make Your Mark in life is to leave a legacy. To know that throughout all the trials and tribulations you've given it your best and have a life of few regrets. There are way too many people in the world who are living on autopilot and hoping that the right opportunity will fall into their lap, and they will miraculously begin living their best life. Unfortunately, it doesn't tend to happen that way.

If today was your last day on earth, can you hand on heart say that you've given it everything that you've got? That you've contributed and given back to the world? We all deserve to live the life we dream and deserve. Bronnie Ware, an Australian author who for years nursed patients in palliative care, wrote the book *The Top Five Regrets of the*

Dying.[2] Bronnie discovered during her time conversing with her patients that one of the biggest regrets people had on their deathbeds was, "I wish I'd had the courage to live a life true to myself, not the life others expected of me." This is the narrative that I could imagine with the few experiences that I faced either personally or with those dearest to me.

Many of us are so worried about what others think of us; lacking the courage to step up and be seen out of fear of looking egotistical or up ourselves – "Who is she to do that or to be that?" We hold ourselves back from being our best selves for a myriad of reasons. The biggest person who ultimately holds us back is ourselves.

Why Making Your Mark Matters Professionally

Whether you are in the workforce or not, we are all experiencing unprecedented change, the likes of which most of us have never seen in our lifetime. The COVID-19 pandemic has provided people the opportunity for self-reflection, a chance to assess if they really are being their best-selves and living their best lives.

Some of the many challenges that we are experiencing in a professional sense include social distancing, working from home and not being able to travel. These challenges have changed how we connect with others (and ourselves) to make an impact. Many of us are now living digitally rather than physically, which inhibits our ability to present

---

2 Bronnie Ware, *The Top Five Regrets of the Dying* (Alexandria: Hay House, 2012).

ourselves in a traditional manner (in-person meetings, networking, shared offices, events). It can be harder to be personable, memorable, and to Make Your Mark in virtual formats.

Also, now more than ever, many people are experiencing multiple role conflict, and many find it difficult to obtain "balance" or work/life integration – parenting and other carer responsibilities, home schooling, lockdowns, relationship breakdowns, returning to work, redundancies or job losses, and emotional and physical burdens. We can easily lose sight of ourselves, our essence and our dreams through being human *doings* rather than human *beings*.

Changes and advances in technology such as artificial intelligence can also impact our employment opportunities. You need to make yourself indispensable and of high worth so that you are sought after for your expertise and the positive impact and change that you can create. It is imperative to leverage your humanness, your best self.

These challenges also highlight the importance of personal brand. We are all a personal brand. A personal brand is how you present yourself and how you show up to the world. It is a combination of your skillset, story, experiences and the talents that are your superpowers. It is what makes you *you* and is what allows you stand out from others, make a positive impact and be memorable (in a good way).

You need to invest in your personal brand to secure your positioning from both a business and personal perspective. Trends, clients, customers, and companies come and go ... but the one thing that will remain is you. You need to own and capitalise on your uniqueness to create the opportunities you deserve.

You are a personal brand whether you like the idea of being one or not. Establishing and growing your personal brand will be a matter of thriving over surviving – both personally and professionally – and the best way to do that is to invest in your personal development, build a solid foundation, get clear around your identity and vision to Make Your Mark.

Do you feel restless, overwhelmed or frustrated? Are you not sure who you are anymore after experiencing life's curveballs? Do you feel like you're being everything to everyone else, but not to yourself? Do you feel as if you've lost sight of yourself, your essence, and your dreams? Do you consider yourself a high-performing person but you still feel like you're not reaching your full potential, that your life isn't being lived to its fullest? Are you thinking, *But how the heck do I even do that when I am already stretched to my limit?*

This series will show you how to Make Your Mark in your business, career and life. I will gently guide you on your Make Your Mark journey to ensure that you are living a life that is true to you.

I want you to draw a line in the sand now ... X marks the spot, today is the day that it all changes for you, and changes for the better. Either physically or in your imagination, draw an X right on the ground in front of you and step into it. You have drawn your mark to the universe to say that you're stepping up; this is a "this is it" moment. When you look back a few years or even just a few months from now you will remember this moment. It's the moment you decided to invest in yourself and to start living your life the way you want.

It's time to feel empowered, inspired and ready to Make Your Mark in the world; to reach your full potential, not for anyone else – but just for you.

INTRODUCTION TO BOOK 1
Make Your Mark

To truly Make Your Mark, whether that's in small everyday ways or on a large, public scale, you need to lay a solid foundation. The foundation to success lies in having clarity around your identity – having a strong sense of self and self-worth, having a vision so that you know where you're going, understanding your unique gifts that you can share with the world, removing fear and limiting beliefs that are holding you back, being aware of imposter syndrome and not falling into the trap of comparing yourself to others. It's knowing your values and core values so that you have integrity and are living congruently. It's using your intuition, tapping into your inner compass so that you are guided along the way to make the best decisions that you possibly can.

Many experiences during our childhood years form and shape our attitudes, values and beliefs – some of which we may not even be conscious of. They can be hard to identify and change later in life but are none the less powerful in our personal and professional lives as adults. It is for these reasons that many of the stories I share within this book are experiences and moments from my childhood years that have helped to authentically inform all that I do.

This book is very personal. It will help you gain clarity on where you have come from, and guide you to what you might need to shape, evolve and change to get to where you want to be. It has some professional focus, but it is your personal lens that needs adjusting to get results.

In this book, I share with you the twelve key steps I continue to follow and revisit each day. It's a continuous journey that I am on where I still stumble and fall, but now I can dust myself off and get back up quicker! I hope that my paving this path and laying this foundation helps you to pave your own path to becoming your best self, building a strong personal/business brand, and determining how you're going to Make Your Mark in the world and how the world might make its mark on you.

Let's get you started with laying your solid foundation to become your best self and to Make Your Mark.

THE MAKE YOUR MARK *Scale*

Level	Obstacle	Focus	MAKE YOUR MARK %
The name of each level to Make Your Mark	The obstacle that can hold you back at each level	This is what your focus needs to be on at each level	The level of impact of Your Mark
THRIVER	CONTINUITY	BEST-SELF	100%
RISER	BALANCE	CONGRUENCE	75%
EXPLORER	FEAR	MINDSET	50%
BELIEVER	VALUE	SELF-BELIEF	30%
SEEKER	CLARITY	IDENTITY	15%
STRIVER	OVERWHELM	DECISION	-10%

Jessica Ritchie ©

You can use the Make Your Mark Scale to identify where you are at on your journey. There are six levels to become your best self and Make Your Mark, going from "Striver" (level 1) to a "Thriver" (level 6).

This is a sliding scale where you move up each level (going left to right). It allows you to discover where you are at now and identify where it is that you want to go on your journey. You can go up and down the scale at times, but your goal is to get to the top of the scale and focus on continuing being your best self, thriving at the top level, and making your mark.

How to use the scale:

Read through the explanations of the levels, and place a mark beside the level that you are at now. Then place another larger mark next to the level where you want to be. As you work through the exercises in this book, you now have an indicator to refer back to when you review your progress!

Level 1 - Striver

At the lowest level of the scale, you feel you are constantly **striving**. You are so **overwhelmed** that you are struggling, and everything seems like a strenuous effort. No mark is being made; in fact, you are flatlining. You are struggling to know where to begin, and so the result is that you're stuck, a little lost and don't know what to do next. You are not operating as your best self, and you are not making your mark. You know you can be more, and you want to leave a legacy. You look at others achieving their personal and professional goals, yet you just don't know how they're doing it. Remaining at this level can be detrimental to your mindset and can lead to feelings of hopelessness. You are tired of this and you need to make the **decision** to seek support to start your journey to get to the next level.

Level 2 - Seeker

At this level, you are the seeker of **clarity** to discover who you are and where it is that you are going. You need clarity first and foremost, with the focus on your **identity**. You are so many things to so many people; you have so many commitments that you've lost your sense of self. Losing yourself can occur through the changes and challenges that life has dealt you, particularly if you haven't taken the time to reflect and take stock of where you're at. You feel like you've been busily treading water, but you're at a point where you can bring your head up to take a breath. But as you look around, you no longer recognise yourself and even your surroundings feel like they might no longer fit. You're thinking, *Who I am? How did I even get here? What is it that I want from life? What gives me joy? What do I need to change?* Now is time to focus on your identity and to get your magic back. This is the point for you to remove the layers of what no longer serves you and rediscover who you truly are to move up to the next level to Make Your Mark.

Level 3 – Believer

At this level, you have clarity around who you are and all that you do by having a rock-solid identity. But you question the **value** that you bring, personally and professionally, which creates a lack of self-worth. You may rely on others cheering for you, basing your worth on external sources. You have everything within you to succeed, you just need to believe it yourself. It's time to be a **believer** in yourself to discover the gifts that you have within you. You may get thrown off course if someone challenges you, and you second guess yourself. You may take others' opinions on board at the expense of your own thoughts and what you believe to be right. This is where you focus on your **self-belief**. You need to **believe** in what you are capable of, what you've done in the past and dig deep within yourself. You now have a strong sense of self, and believing in what you can do and achieve is what elevates you to the next level on your journey. Through reviewing and considering your skillsets, your life experience, what you are known for, and your ability to adapt to change (including the story of your life up to this point), you start to understand what it is that makes you unique. This awareness strengthens your self-belief. Your uniqueness forms part of your magic. Your uniqueness bolsters your worth. By cultivating high self-esteem and self-worth, you leave no doubt in your mind what you can offer the world. You will no longer sell yourself short or undercharge your worth. By knowing your worth, you ensure that your community, workplace, friends and family know the value that you bring, too!

Level 4 – Explorer

At this level you are at 50% to making your mark! You have cultivated a strong identity, you have clarity, and you know the value you bring coupled with a strong mindset and vision. The obstacle that you are now finding is that **fear** gets in the way of your progress, and you start to slow down. It's time to become an **explorer** into what exactly is holding you back. Be curious and creative on this quest of self-discovery. Imposter syndrome has come to visit, and you might be having thoughts like, *Who are am I to be doing this? Who am I to be this person? What if I am not good enough? What if I get found out?!* Limiting beliefs that have been with you for years and that no longer serve are brought to the forefront. Testing you to see how much you really want to pave your path and put yourself out there. Comparisonitis to others in your industry, friendship groups, family and society absorbs a lot of your time and produces self-doubt. On their own and combined, these thoughts are holding you back from making your mark. Strengthening your **mindset** is what is required, and reaching deep within your reserves to overcome these challenges and bring yourself into the here and now. It's time to explore within (not looking for external praise) and harness your capabilities. You know deep down that you've got this. You do believe in yourself and your abilities otherwise you wouldn't be at this level. You've come too far to give up now!

Level 5 – Riser

At this level you are really getting a sense of how you can Make Your Mark personally and professionally. At times though, you may feel like you are out of **balance** as you juggle the many roles and tasks required of you daily. You're operating at 75% and the closer you get to making your mark the more the momentum builds, and your impact and ability to stand out in the world – for all the right reasons – starts to speed up. It is a balancing act of trying not to lose control of what matters most over things that matter least. You will be tested and challenged by not only others but yourself to remain true to who you are. Your focus is to develop your intuition and to trust your instincts. This aids in quicker (and generally more successful) decision-making. As you put this into practice, you will find yourself **rise** above things that in the past would have weighed you down. You are on a mission and your values and instincts are acting as a compass that is guiding you on your vision to leave a legacy. Maintaining your integrity at all times and being your most authentic self allows you to be **congruent** in all that you do. It takes the pressure off, allows for more joy and flow in your life and gives you confidence that you know what you have to do to Make Your Mark and fulfill your potential. It is time to go to the next level by stepping into your personal power to become your best self.

Level 6 – Thriver

At the top of the scale is where you Make Your Mark! Your challenge at this level is retaining the **continuity** and cadence of all the hard work and building blocks that you've created in the prior levels. You must keep going and integrate all the key elements to Make Your Mark, focusing on performance and embedding your personal development. You are **thriving** and no longer striving and surviving, you are standing out from the crowd and presenting your most confident and authentic self. The result of the continuation of your work is becoming your **best self**. Being your best self means that you aren't easily distracted or deterred by the challenges that come your way. You are so rock-solid in your identity, belief in yourself and the value that you provide; you have a powerful mindset that's in alignment and congruent with your most authentic self. Your best self provides maximum impact at 100% to create your legacy and Make Your Mark in business, career and most importantly, life. It's time to confidently pave your path and lead the way so that others can follow your light!

STEP 1

Identity & Sense of Self

> "Find your identity, your true self and live your mission ... Your power is your radical self. Find it."
>
> — AYA CHEBBI

I woke up one morning deciding it was time to inject some colour, energy and life back into my garden. As I looked out my window, I could see that the garden was so dry that the soil was cracked in places. The once thriving plants were beaten and weathered from the sun. There were weeds scattered across the lawn, and dead leaves tucked into every crevice of the garden.

In that moment, I realised that to fulfill my vision of a blooming, colourful and thriving garden, I needed to nurture the foundation upon which my garden would sustainably grow. Without a healthy, solid foundation, I was wasting my time, energy and money.

I toiled the earth and placed new soil and mulch into the garden. I planted the seedlings, added some supercharged fertiliser to nourish their health and I watered them, day after day – sometimes twice per day.

And as I pondered the moments of reflection that gardening provides, I came to understand that I wanted to fully bloom myself. The time, effort and care that I was bestowing upon my garden needed to be bestowed upon me. I wanted to make my mark in my business, career and life – but first I needed a solid foundation in order to do that, and really, could it be that different to tending to a garden?

Having a **strong sense of self** is the first step to building the foundation for our success. It's like fresh, healthy, well-fertilised soil in a garden. Maya Angelou, an acclaimed American poet, storyteller, activist, and autobiographer who was also Hollywood's first black female director, once made the link between a strong sense of self, identity, and success really clear, saying that "Success is liking yourself, liking what you do, and liking how you do it."

What Is Sense of Self?

The American Psychological Association defines sense of self as our feeling of "identity, uniqueness and self-direction".[3] Having a strong sense of self is the first key to building a solid foundation. Your sense of self is important because you are living in a time of unprecedented change, increased demands within your home and workplace, conflicting deadlines, unexpected curveballs, life challenges and experiences. And don't forget about the many roles that you play in life.

If you don't have a strong sense of self, I reckon it can be a bit like not having an EPIRB (an emergency position-indicating radio beacon, used to alert search and rescue services in the event of an emergency) when you're out exploring unknown territory. You don't have the ability to send an SOS call or send up a spark of light to help others find you. You need to find yourself before others can truly help you.

But what if I do not even know who I am?

I hear you. It takes guts to think or say that. I've had the privilege of working with hundreds of clients in my

---

[3] *APA Dictionary of Psychology,* s.v. "Sense of self," accessed October 12, 2021, https://dictionary.apa.org/sense-of-self.

business, many of them with a low sense of self who say that they don't know who they are at all, or don't know who they are anymore. I admire their vulnerability. They talk about feeling overwhelmed, disconnected, and lost. Because of this, they lack confidence to try new things, go for promotions, or start something new. They are frustrated that they can't make their mark, yet they know that they deserve to. One of the resounding comments that I hear is, "I don't know who I truly am." Yes, I have felt like that; I have been there too.

I have found that women quite often say something like this after taking long service leave or a lengthy holiday, during or after maternity leave, or after an extended period of time being a carer to a relative or a friend. Men have shared that they feel lost after having their first child while trying to be "super dad" – being the family provider, coming to terms with their new role and responsibility as a father, all while supporting their partner mentally and emotionally.

Sometimes people say they don't know themselves after a significant life event that has forced them to think and reflect: when they are recovering from ill health; after a traumatic scare or accident; if their marriage ends; when their children start going to school or eventually leave home; or during global events such as pandemics or terrorism. Women in particular are often so busy being everything to everyone else that they can lose themselves and their identity in the chaos of life.

So what can I do about that?

In order to have a strong sense of self, it's imperative that you have **clarity** around who you truly are and what it is that makes you unique. What does this clarity entail?

- You need to be **self-aware** – understanding where you're at and how you're feeling, and acknowledging these.

- You need to **like yourself** – including what you perceive as your quirks and flaws, because that is what sets you apart from competitors and all the "sameness" that is in the world.

- You need to be **confident** in your identity, in all that you are – this is your secret weapon to flourish as a flower when you might feel like a bunch of unwanted weeds.

- You need to **like and enjoy** what it is that you do in your business, career and life – this creates an **energy and vibe** that becomes infectious. Your vibe is what helps you achieve your vision, and connect with the people who can help and support you. It also allows you to retain quality people in your life. If you're in business or a leader, your vibe and energy is what attracts (and retains) your team members, customers and clients.

- ✗ You need **courage** to step up and to step out – to be seen and to let your voice be heard. Authenticity and realness come with being comfortable with your identity. It allows you to be confident in asking for what you want, going for opportunities to achieve your vision, and getting results.

By having a **strong sense of self**, you can be more resistant to the challenges that pop up at us in life – whether they're small pebbles, rocks, or huge boulders. The challenges can come from other people in our lives, or from situations we face that test us. A strong identity amplifies your self-awareness and resilience. These attributes allow you to keep momentum rather than shrivelling and withering away when challenges (like droughts and storms for gardens) occur throughout your life.

Do You Have A Strong Identity to Set A Solid Foundation to Make Your Mark?

In a world where you need to be more agile than ever, you simply can't afford to have cracks appear in your foundation. You must be aware of the needs that you require for yourself first and foremost, so that you are able to bloom in all your glory, and Make Your Mark.

I don't know about you, but I witness a lot of "copy and paste" behaviour in today's world. And it just doesn't stick (with me, anyway). It doesn't hit the mark. I find it sad because it means that those people are not taking the time to discover what it is that makes them unique; they lack the confidence to be themselves. They think it's easier to be under the guise of someone else, trying to emulate and emanate their essence. You can tell that they don't have their own story. Trying to be someone else not only has a detrimental and damaging effect on a person's personal or business brand, but ultimately also to their sense of self, which impacts every part of their life. With a strong identity and sense of self, you will have the clarity and confidence to be your most authentic, unique self to Make Your Mark.

The positive effects of having a strong identity flow into our business and workplaces too. A survey by global strategy consulting company Strategy& revealed that companies with a strong identity were more likely to outperform other businesses by 25%.[4] A strong identity, in this survey, was defined as a company "knowing themselves well and leveraging their distinctive strengths ... [and] standing for something unique and consistent over time".[5] This could easily be the definition of an individual with a strong identity: when you know yourself well, understand your strengths and how to use them, and know your values – consistently and authentically!

With the rise in competition for customers and clients (and their hard earned dollars), it is imperative that leaders

---

4 Strategy&, *What Drives A Company's Success? Highlights of Survey Findings* (New York: PricewaterhouseCoopers, 2013), https://www.strategyand.pwc.com/gx/en/insights/2002-2013/what-drives-a-companys-success/strategyand-what-drives-a-companys-success.pdf.
5 Strategy&, *What Drives A Company's Success?*, 3.

not only look to their personal and professional identities, but also to the identity of the company they lead, to the identities of their employees, and to the identities of their customers and clients. A clear understanding of these different identities, and the relationship between them, allow people to feel valued, heard, and that genuine connections are being made. If leaders do this, they will strike an enviable unique competitive advantage simply by focusing on the power of identity.

What Strategy Do You Have In Place To Ensure That You Will Fully Bloom?

If you check in with yourself on a regular basis to get the basics right, then you will develop a solid foundation for your personal and professional growth.

The basics required to strengthen sense of self are:

1. **Get clarity** by taking some time to stop and reflect and ask yourself the questions:
   - *Who am I? What are the roles I have in my life?*
   - *What is that I want to do?*
   - *Am I living my best life?*
   - *What is holding me back from living my best life?*
   - *What are my fears?*
   - *Are my fears valid? (i.e. what is the likelihood of my fear really occurring?)*
   - *What is that I enjoy?*
   - *How often do I get to do what I enjoy?*

- What do I need to change so that I can do more of what I enjoy?

2. **Start nourishing your mind and body** with the basics – such as eating good, clean, healthy food, drinking plenty of fresh filtered water, moving your body through exercise (by whatever means is enjoyable for you), and getting quality sleep.

3. **Make yourself a priority.** Be sure that you take the time to do activities that bring you joy. Quite often these are the first things that fall by the wayside when life gets busy or tough. It's so important for your sense of self to dedicate time each day (it doesn't have to be a long amount of time) to something that brings you joy, allows you to switch off, removes the busy-ness and connects you back into yourself. One way to make yourself a priority is to set a reminder alarm or mark out time in your diary (like you would for a doctor's appointment) so this becomes a non-negotiable. You do not move or delete your appointment with yourself! (I know I used to and trust me, it's not good when you keep doing it!). The activity you choose to prioritise yourself might be something as simple as running a bath and lighting a candle once a week (this is one of mine!).

4. **Practice gratitude, mindfulness and meditation.** These activities are like the fertiliser for your garden. Start by introducing these into your routine, even if

only for a few minutes each day or each week. They will make you feel more grounded and balanced, and you will most certainly notice the benefits that they provide in all that you do.

5. **Remove what or who is not serving you** for your best and highest good. These activities or people are like weeds in your garden – they drain you of your energy, and continue to take and take from you but never give anything in return. If it's not as easy as simply cutting the activity or person from your life, slowly start to distance yourself and put some boundaries in place to protect yourself and your energy.

6. **A daily dose of fresh air and sunshine** should never be underestimated. Take the time to go outside, close your eyes, take some deep, meaningful breathes to slow down your heart rate, and just feel the warmth of the sun on your face, feel the gentle breeze on your skin. Again, it's about connecting back into yourself and just allowing some space to "just be". Like flowers need the warmth of the sun to grow, so do you.

7. **Adopt a routine and discipline** that works for *you*. Look to incorporating the above steps each and every day. Keep toiling the soil, adding fertiliser, removing weeds and watering your garden each day in order for your foundation to remain strong and for it to grow and blossom.

8. **Keep checking back in** with yourself and asking yourself how you're going so that your sense of self – your identity – remains strong and continues to be the foundation to your success in business, career and life.

It is time for you to Make Your Mark through having a strong identity and sense of self!

MAKE YOUR MARK
Moment

In 2016, just after I had my second child, I was feeling lost. We had moved to a very small town in regional Queensland, Australia, called Helidon for my husband Sam's work. We had few to no local friends, a six-week-old baby, Billy, and a toddler, Max, in tow. I was still processing the death of one of my best friends, Naomi, to ovarian cancer, the death of another close friend, Frankie, to pancreatic cancer, and an accident that left one of my dear brothers, Nathan, paralysed on Easter Sunday. I was pondering and questioning the meaning of life and what my purpose was supposed to be. I was confused and grieving, adapting to being a mum of two in a new home and community. I was taking one day at a time to go through the motions and emotions. Despite all that I had to deal with, I was also feeling a restlessness that I wanted to do more and be more *because* of those difficult experiences, but what? I had no clue.

    Fast forward to the 29th of May, 2017. I woke in the morning feeling uneasy. My breathing was shallow, and I needed to keep pacing the perimeter of my garden as I could not stay still. I was playing outside with Max and Billy when I heard multiple sirens zoom past – marked and unmarked police cars screeching at high speed through our small town where my husband Sam was (at the time) one of only two police officers. Sam's car was not one of the cars screeching by. I heard the PolAir helicopters hovering and then ambulances. I knew something was dreadfully wrong. I went inside and my phone had numerous missed calls from numbers that I did not know. I called one back and it was a friend of Sam's, Gordon, who was in distress. He said he was watching the news headlines, and kept asking if Sam was OK. I didn't understand what he meant, and he told me to turn on the TV. There on the breaking news headline was: "Police Officer Father of Two, Shot and Killed Near Helidon." With only two officers in Helidon, and my husband's boss being a father of three, I truly thought that Sam was not coming home.

It took forty minutes before I heard from Sam that he was OK; he had been shot at, but it was another officer from a nearby town who had sadly been killed. To feel in every cell of my body the grief and loss of my loved one and my best mate shook me to my core. When I finally heard from Sam, I felt intense gratitude and blessings that he was OK, but this was coupled with immense guilt and shame – someone had still lost their life, and their loved ones were grieving. It was like a "back from the dead" moment that's hard to describe.

I had a lot of other life experiences that enabled me to keep as calm as possible and remain focused during the day of that incident, especially during those forty minutes when I didn't know if Sam had been hurt. I didn't want Max and Billy to know what was happening and for it to affect them. But after a few days, as the enormity of it all started to sink in, I began to feel wobbly. This wasn't supposed to be about me. I wasn't the one shot at. I hadn't lost my husband. I was safe. But our minds allow us to go to the very depths of the "what ifs" that we live the stories anyway. Combined with my already shaky sense of self, I asked my mother-in-law Rhonda to mind the boys so I could take some time out. I was concerned about Sam and felt guilty that I was feeling so much when he was the one that had literally had numerous bullets fired at him. Yet, I couldn't deny nor downplay what I was feeling.

To be honest, I had downplayed my feelings for most of my life and I knew if I was to do that again now, I would find myself in even bigger trouble – mentally, physically, emotionally and spiritually. Instinctively, I went to my mirror. I looked long and hard at my reflection. I remember staring at my face and soaking in all its features, like a stranger to myself. I then said, without thinking, "Hello, how are you going, buddy?" And I cried ... and I cried. Hearing myself call myself "buddy" with such kindness and care is what allowed the waterworks. I hadn't been kind to myself for a long time, I'd been "keeping on keeping on", not allowing myself to feel or even think about it. Many of the events from the past came cascading out of me, unhealed and wanting to be felt and heard. It felt good to release the emotion, to let it go.

I do remember that I felt a bit silly speaking to myself and a small internal voice saying, "Maybe you should stop!", but I spoke to myself with the love and compassion of that for a dear friend and I just kept on going. Looking at myself in the mirror, I had a conversation (out loud) with myself, about how I didn't know who I was any more, and that I was scared. It was a hard conversation. I laid my cards out on the table so that I was no longer hiding from myself. I removed my superwoman cape, my mask, my armour. I was bare. I was vulnerable. I was brave. I let go of the feelings that I felt, that "this situation is not about you, get on with it, you're lucky so move on, you shouldn't feel like this, you weren't there, others feel worse ...", all the stories that I was telling myself. I had a right to feel what I felt without dismissing it.

What that experience re-affirmed to me was that I knew more than ever that life was too damn short to not grab it with both hands. It was a wakeup call for me to **live**. It was time to follow my heart. To do the things that I'd wanted to do but had been too afraid. To do whatever the heck I wanted to do with my life. For years I had wanted to study energy healing and neurolinguistic programming, and integrate those skills into my marketing business. I had been so fearful of what others would think of me, that I was "woo woo" or weird, and I feared failure, that I might not be able to integrate it into my business successfully.

After experiencing the benefits of having courageous conversations and checking in with myself on a regular basis, I no longer had that fear. I no longer cared what people thought. I stopped listening to advice from those who hadn't walked in my shoes, and didn't know where I had been and where I was going. I went and learnt and immersed myself in what I had always wanted. From the day that I integrated reiki energy healing, life coaching and neurolinguistic programming into my brand and marketing business, I haven't looked back. It was the best thing that I have done in being true to me and who I am. It is what sets me apart in my industry. I am living my passion and purpose. It allows me to help myself on a daily basis. It allows me to help others on a daily basis. It is one of the ways that I make my mark.

> *"If you are searching for that one person who will change your life, take a look in the mirror."*
> — UNKNOWN

Make Your Markercise

Throughout this book, there are exercises and activities for you to do that will help you Make Your Mark. These are called "Make Your Markercises".

Mirror Mirror:

Take the time to look at yourself in the mirror and check in with yourself on a regular basis. Ideally, try to do this once per week, allowing two to five minutes each time. Yes, it might feel weird the first few times, but you will soon get the hang of it.

This is an exercise in vulnerability requiring the removal of armour. It's incredibly powerful baring your soul to your own self. It's liberating when we allow ourselves the time to open up and release what is not serving us. To hear what we have to say. To listen. To have a conversation where we speak lovingly, compassionately, and with empathy (like we would to a good friend) to ourselves.

Even if you find it difficult, don't give up the first time. Keep going with it. Start by checking in with yourself for one minute, even if you speak no words; allow yourself to feel comfortable taking in the details of your face and what feelings might be coming through. Have the intention to work your way towards increasing the time you spend doing this exercise to dig a bit deeper, getting to really know yourself and building up your understanding of your identity and sense of self. Don't give up, keep going!

SENSE OF *Self*
SUN SYSTEM

Jessica Ritchie ©

When I started putting together a system to explain sense of self, I realised that the system reminded me of the sun. This comparison seemed so accurate, because when we have a balanced, strong sense of self, we shine bright like the sun on a perfect summer's day. But just like if the sun's rays disappear behind a cloud, if any of the rays in your Sense of Self Sun System (SOSSS) are taken away, you can lose your shine, your light, and your ability to burn bright to Make Your

Mark. Conversely, if you have too much in a particular sunray compared to the others, your sense of self could become unbalanced, overloaded and may even burn you out in that particular area.

This is why there are double arrows in the SOSSS that go out from you and back to you for each sunray. It's important to remember that energy is exchanged in every interaction, and I want you to take the time to reflect on the energy that you give and what is given back to you in return. This provides the best indicator of where you are at and what changes may need to be made to strengthen your sense of self.

Ready to begin?

Take the time to rate out of ten (with ten being the highest) the amount of satisfaction that you have in each area of the sense of self system. These are the areas that I've identified as the most popular from what I have seen with my clients. You are welcome to substitute or add in any areas that you wish. It is powerful to make a detailed list beside each area about what makes up each of those rays of light for you. For example, "family" could be made up of your mother, daughter, nephew, cousin and dog. You can even go as far as thinking about where each person within your family sits on the scale out of ten.

Listing out what is within each facet allows you to get a true sense of all that it encompasses, and a true sense of yourself. I have provided some prompts for each area to help get you started. It is up to you how in-depth you wish to take this exercise, but you may get more value from it by going deeper.

Family

- List all the roles that you have within the "family" ray. Perhaps you're a partner, mother, step-mother, daughter, niece, sister, sister-in-law, *and* an aunty. If you're a member of a blended family, you might have even more roles.
- Think about the different roles and titles that you have and the commitment, expectations and energy required with each.
- Are there any roles that are easier than others? Are any harder than others? Why?
- Is there anything within your control that you can do to improve how you feel about or show up in that role?

Out of ten, how satisfied are you in this area?   /10

Work

- Do you currently work? If not, do you want to work?
- What is the role that you have? Is it the role or career that you want? Are you happy with your work and what you do?
- Is something holding you back from the career or job you want?
- Do you have balance in place so your work is not all-consuming?
- Do you want to give back to your industry by volunteering or mentoring others?

Out of ten, how satisfied are you in this area?   /10

Hobbies

- What do you do in your spare time for pleasure and leisure?
- Are there any hobbies you would like to do more of?
- Which activities bring you the most joy?
- Is there anything holding you back from doing hobbies you enjoy or trying new ones?

Out of ten, how satisfied are you in this area?   /10

Values[6]

- What are your values? What are your core values?
- Are your values being met?
- How are you living your values every day?

Out of ten, how satisfied are you in this area?   /10

Finances

- Do you feel comfortable with your financial situation? Does it keep you up at night with worry or do you feel at ease?
- Are you able to pay your bills on time?
- Do you have sufficient savings if you are faced with an emergency? Do you have savings so you can treat yourself?
- Do you have superannuation and know how much you need to feel comfortable in retirement?
- Are you comfortable seeking financial advice if you need it?

---

6 Please see Step 9 for more information on values and core values, and how to identify these.

✗ Are you being paid what you are worth in your job? If not, is there an opportunity to ask for a pay rise, or should you be considering different career opportunities?

Out of ten, how satisfied are you in this area?   /10

Health

✗ Do you keep up with recommended physical health checks with medical professionals? Do you have an annual physical with your GP, yearly or twice-yearly check-ups with your dentist and optometrist?

✗ What activities do you do to maintain your physical health? Do you engage in regular exercise, drink plenty of filtered water each day, and nourish yourself with healthy food?

✗ What activities do you do to maintain your mental health? Do you practice mindfulness and meditation? Do you seek support from a qualified expert if you have mental health concerns?

✗ Is there anything holding you back from ensuring your health is at its best?

Out of ten, how satisfied are you in this area?   /10

Culture

✗ Think about the elements of your culture that are important to you. These might be traditions, rituals, customs, or beliefs that are personal and individual to you, followed just in your family, or shared between a large community. Culture may also include food, history, language, art, music, and behaviour.

- Which elements of your culture do you enjoy? Which do you dislike?
- Are there any elements of your culture you'd like to engage with more often? Or less often?

Out of ten, how satisfied are you in this area?   /10

Goals

- What are your goals in life? Do you have goals for the short-, medium-, and long-term in your life?
- What are you doing to work towards reaching your goals? Do you do anything that makes it harder for you to reach your goals?
- Are your goals truly your own, or are they goals other people want for you?

Out of ten, how satisfied are you in this area?   /10

Friends

- Do you have at least two good friends who you can be vulnerable with? Good friends are reliable, supportive, loyal, non-judgemental, honest, trustworthy, and are willing to challenge you when needed.
- Are you a good friend?
- How often do you catch up with friends to "fill your cup"? Would you prefer to socialise more, or less often?

Out of ten, how satisfied are you in this area?   /10

Spirituality

✘ Think about spiritual elements that are important to you. This might be as part of a traditional, organised religion, or a personal relationship with your own soul and spirit.

✘ How do you express and explore your connection to your soul and spirit? Do you meditate, journal, spend time in nature, pray, or serve your community?

✘ Are there any activities you'd like to do more of to engage with your spirit?

Out of ten, how satisfied are you in this area?   /10

Collate your scores from each of the SOSSS rays to work out your overall score and to make it easier to compare which areas are performing and shining strongly and which areas might be feeling dull and a little grey.

Sense of Self Sun System Ray	Score
Family	/10
Work	/10
Hobbies	/10
Values	/10
Finances	/10
Health	/10
Culture	/10
Goals	/10
Friends	/10
Spirituality	/10
Overall Score:	**/100**

The SOSSS helps you to make any necessary changes to solidify your identity and to remove any elements dulling your shine. You can see where your energy is going and who and what may be consuming it. It allows each facet of you to shine bright like a diamond (or the sun in this case) to enable you to Make Your Mark.

STEP 2

Self-Worth – Know Your Worth

"You're always with yourself, so you might as well enjoy the company."

— DIANE VON FURSTENBERG

Many people use the terms "self-esteem" and "self-worth" synonymously, but they are different – they are closely related concepts that work hand-in-hand with and influence one another. Self-worth is the core belief a person has about their intrinsic value as a person, that they are necessary and worthy of love and success; while self-esteem is a broader opinion someone has of themselves – the combination of how they view, think and feel about themselves – which includes their belief about their self-worth. Self-esteem has been defined as "the degree to which the qualities and characteristics contained in one's self-concept [such as self-worth] are perceived to be positive."[7] The better a person's sense of self-worth, the higher their self-esteem is likely to be.

I think of self-worth to be a bit like a money box. When I was a child, I would get so excited if my money box was heavy. It meant that it had lots of coins in it! But what I've learnt, through the wisdom that comes with age and life experience, is that I would much prefer a money box full of notes rather than a handful of coins. The money box full of notes might feel a lot lighter, and from outside observation might seem to be worth a lot less than a box containing heavy coins. Lightness and high worth can propel you much further than the heaviness and lower value of coins. If you base your self-worth on outside perceptions of your value, you might be led astray, and not realise your actual worth.

---

[7] *APA Dictionary of Psychology*, s.v. "Sense-esteem," accessed October 12, 2021, https://dictionary.apa.org/self-esteem.

> *"Over the years, I've interviewed thousands of people, most of them women, and I would say that the root of every dysfunction I've ever encountered, every problem, has been some sense of a lacking self-value or of self-worth."*
> — OPRAH WINFREY

Why do some of us struggle with our worth and the value that we bring?

Have you ever thought something like, *How did I even get to this position in a company?* Or, *How did I build this business?* Or even, *Who do I think that I am wanting to do and be it all?* At times we can think that we do not deserve success because of beliefs we have about ourselves, or imposter syndrome (which we will talk about shortly) might make us feel like a fraudster.

Many people base their worth on all kinds of external matters, such as how many friends they have, what suburb they live in, their salary or the amount of money they earn in business, or their physical appearance – how young and sexy they might look. These are all trivial matters (when perspective comes into play), but it is easy to get caught up in external stimuli and start to believe that all of that matters if our sense of self-worth is low. Self-worth is about knowing, loving, and valuing exactly who you are, not about what you think you should be, or what you have.

"You have been criticizing yourself for years, and it hasn't worked. Try approving of yourself and see what happens."
— LOUISE L. HAY

Know, Like and Trust Yourself

Business leaders and authors Bob Burg and Zig Ziglar have both been famously quoted as saying something like you need to have people know, like and trust you in order for them to listen to you and want to do business with you. But I believe that we need to rewind a little and first ask, "Do you know, like, and trust **yourself?**"

If you don't know yourself or like yourself, you need to increase your self-esteem. Stop relying on external influences to bolster how you perceive yourself. Dig deep and know the worth that you bring: you've earned it, you deserve it. You then need to further boost your self-perception with the trust factor of self-worth – where you love yourself for who you are, which brings confidence to back yourself. If *you* don't understand and value your worth, how can you expect others to value it? You need to be and lead yourself first, before you can lead and inspire others.

Once you achieve this and you know, like and trust yourself, you can then build authentic, connected personal and business brands in your workplace, and with your teams, customers, and clients. You will become more aligned and congruent in your identity with integrity and purpose. It will allow you to shine bright like the sun and Make Your Mark.

How to know, like and trust yourself:

Know yourself:

- ✖ Figure out if you have been basing your self-worth on internal or external matters. Have superficial things like your clothing size become more important to your self-worth than your internal values?

- ✖ Develop a strong sense of self (use the SOSSS from Step 1).

- ✖ Assess your habits. Develop habits that increase and extend the value that you bring to yourself and others. Discard unhelpful habits.

Like yourself:

- ✖ Embrace your perceived flaws and love who you are as a whole being. Remind yourself that you are human, after all. You are allowed to make mistakes. We are most often our own biggest critic, but give yourself the same grace you give others.

- ✖ Practice self-compassion and self-care so that you speak kindly to yourself. Have perspective with the inner dialogues you have. You most likely tell others to be kind. It's time to be kind to yourself.

Trust yourself:

- ✘ Remind yourself that you were made to do incredible things and to stand out from the crowd. It's time to back yourself; you've got this. Trust that all is unfolding as it should. It's your time to shine.

- ✘ Keep a folder or file of testimonials you've received from friends, family, colleagues and clients. Read them to remind and affirm to yourself of the high-quality work that you have brought and continue to bring. This might seem counterintuitive as you shouldn't rely on external influences for your value. However, when you sincerely need reminding of what you have achieved or how much you mean to people, this can be a powerful exercise.

By cultivating your self-worth, you increase your confidence and courage and bolster your self-esteem to deserving heights.

Make Your Markercise

THE *Self-Worth* QUADRANT

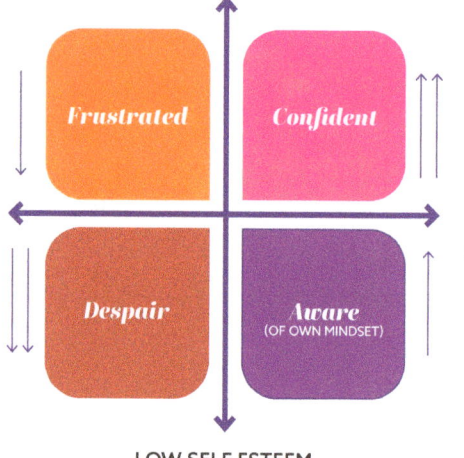

HIGH SELF ESTEEM

High Self Esteem and Trust in Inner Guidance
= 2x Faster to Recover from a Hit

EXTERNAL INFLUENCE

Listens and Acts
Upon Others
Opinions or Beliefs

INTERNAL INFLUENCE

Listen to Inner Voice
+ Trust Own
Guidance System

Frustrated | *Confident*
Despair | *Aware* (OF OWN MINDSET)

LOW SELF ESTEEM

Low Self Esteem and Reliant on Input from Others
= 2x Harder Fall from a Hit/Challenge

Jessica Ritchie ©

Are you wanting to expand your self-worth and self-esteem through increased awareness and confidence? Are you ready to break free of the constraints of external influences that leave you frustrated or in a state of despair? Do you feel you have limited space to grow and evolve your worth? Is it time to focus on feeling light with high value, like the money box that we spoke about earlier? The Self-Worth Quadrant is a useful tool to identify how strong your sense of self-worth and self-esteem are, and what you might need to work on. It is time to move into the Confident quadrant, to step into your personal power and own your worth.

There are four positions in the Self-Worth Quadrant:

CONFIDENT: You feel **confident** when you have high self-esteem and your self-worth and internal dialogue is kept high, light and positive. You have a strong mindset, display courage and are resilient. You are not afraid of failure and have the ability to trust your intuition (inner guidance) and back yourself. When you do take a "hit" or experience a challenge, you recover twice as fast as those in the Despair quadrant. You are not relying on external sources or stimuli to boost your confidence or your value; you have your mindset in the right place to Make Your Mark as you know that it all stems from within.

AWARE: You are **aware** that your internal dialogue that is speaking to your self-worth is generally positive, and you trust your own guidance system. You may lack some courage to step up in certain situations and understand the true value that you bring. This must be realised to increase your self-esteem to a higher order, and to increase your confidence in your work and life.

FRUSTRATED: You can feel **frustrated** when you have a high self-esteem and know the worth that you bring, yet you still find yourself listening to external sources who really aren't worth listening to. This brings self-doubt and decision-making based on other's opinions and beliefs.

DESPAIR: You can feel **despair** when you are in a place of low self-worth and low self-esteem. This is because you are taking on the opinions and beliefs of others as to what you should be doing or who you should be. It feels all-encompassing and you aren't quite sure how to shift your state. The Despair quadrant is where you rely on input from others and when challenges occur, you can fall twice as hard than those who are confident. It's time to switch off listening to the opinions of others who you really don't care for and start to gently guide yourself towards cultivating self-compassion and care for yourself first and foremost, remembering the value that you bring to yourself and to others.

1. Once you've read the description of each part of the Self-Worth Quadrant, identify where you are currently sitting.
2. If you're in any quadrant besides Confident, ask yourself the following questions:
    - Are you listening to external dialogue that does not serve you? Where or who is this coming from? How can you challenge this?
    - Are you listening to positive internal dialogue? Make a list of times you've trusted your intuition with a successful outcome.
    - Is your self-esteem high (in the Frustrated quadrant) or low (in the Despair quadrant)? If it's low, what strategies can you use to boost your self-esteem?
    - What can you do in your life to increase your self-esteem and your self-worth?

MAKE YOUR MARK
Moment

I think the five cent coin gets a bit of a rough time. The Australian government talks about taking it out of circulation, and people can't be bothered to bend over and pick it up off the floor when they drop one. I was on maternity leave with my first son, Max, and money was becoming tight. The company I worked for went into liquidation and the payments that I was entitled to (and that we had budgeted for) ceased immediately. Suddenly, we were most certainly having to watch every penny.

One particular day, I was grocery shopping at rush hour and was mentally calculating the cost of each item. I knew exactly how much money we had in our bank account, down to the last cent. Once I was at the register, I swiped my card and it declined. I realised with utter embarrassment that I was five cents short. Five cents. The five cent piece that I'd seen countless times on the floor of a shop, or that'd rolled out of the car unnoticed, or been discarded in a gutter. The coin that I had never been bothered to pick up, because I didn't believe that it held value.

With people tapping their feet impatiently behind me and Max screaming in the pram, I had to quickly decide which staple I had to remove. I suddenly had a new respect for the five cent coin.

The face value of the situation I was in was five cents, but the REAL value was my own self-worth which had hit a new low. Having gone from earning a very healthy salary in my corporate job to earning no income at all had impacted my self-worth and esteem at that time. I hadn't realised until then. In that very moment, I felt like a failure, and I had guilt and shame that I could not provide for my family like I could when I was working. My pride was hurt, and my self-confidence diminished.

After reflecting on the experience some days later, I came to realise that my ego and a set of beliefs that were no longer serving me were talking. To shift my self-worth and internal dialogue to a healthy state, I thought about all the times that I had contributed financially for my family, but also about how my work at home was priceless and not to be undervalued just because I wasn't being "paid" for being a mother. I welcomed self-compassion and acknowledged that I was a good mum, wife, provider and person, and that this was only a temporary situation that I had found myself in. And so I expressed gratitude for that. I realised how blessed I had been to not have struggled financially on a daily basis before.

So, just how some may underestimate the value in a five cent coin, don't underestimate your own self-worth like I was doing. Don't just take things at face value. Know your worth. Know the value you bring to your work, family, and life. And never underestimate yourself. You are priceless, precious and of immeasurable worth. Believe it! YOU ARE WORTH IT! (And just so you know, now when I see a five cent coin, I **always** pick it up. As the saying goes: see a penny, pick it up, and all that day you'll have good luck.)

STEP 3

Vision – Permission to Dream

> *"First, think. Second, believe. Third, dream. And finally, dare."*
>
> — WALT DISNEY

Are you ready to lead your business, career and life with vision, passion and purpose?

Your vision, when it is clear, allows you to be in the director's chair of *your* work and life. I don't know about you, but I can recall times when I've thought, *STOP!* When I just wanted to pause in this moment, or rewind into the past or fast forward into the future. **You are the main character in your film of life.** When coaching emerging leaders or high-performing women, I find that many need to remember *that they are also* the sole director and producer of their life. This is true for you as well. You have the power to step up and to take charge. It is time to take that elevated seat as director and own it!

When you have crystal-clear **vision** of where you want to go and who you want to be, it provides **a stage to be brave.** Your vision allows you to direct where you are going. It provides a sense of awareness of the story that you are creating, with the big picture in the forefront of your mind.

Walt Disney is a great inspiration to me when it comes to vision and dreams. He had been passionate about drawing since he was very young, and studied art and cartoon drawing. One of his first jobs was as a cartoonist for the *Kansas City Star* newspaper, but he was soon fired because the editor thought Walt "lacked imagination and had no good ideas."[8] Then the first animation film studio he opened, Laugh-O-Gram Studios, went bankrupt. But these early set-backs didn't stop him from following his vision,

---

8 Roger Conners and Tom Smith, *The Wisdom of Oz* (New York: Portfolio/Penguin, 2014), chapter 8.

and he moved to Hollywood and founded another studio (which would later become the Walt Disney Company). After experimenting with other animal cartoon characters, Walt Disney created Mickey Mouse. The eventual success of Mickey Mouse, and Disney's commitment to new technology in animation, led to him creating more and more popular and award-winning cartoons and movies. From these humble beginnings, all from one clear vision and dream, Disney was able to build an empire; winning a record twenty-two Academy Awards and opening beloved theme parks around the world like Disneyland, the "Happiest Place on Earth". Walt Disney's clear vision of himself as an artist and cartoonist, despite the setbacks he faced, led him to become one of the most enduring producers, pioneers, and providers of entertainment of all time. If Disney hadn't been so clear with his vision and belief, who knows where his life may have led – and how different the world might be? As Disney himself said, "I only hope that we don't lose sight of one thing – that it was all started by a mouse." May we all live with the same courage and conviction as Walt Disney to pursue our dreams!

Foresight and Forethought

All too often I see people, women in particular, take a step back from the spotlight because they feel more comfortable and content in supporting roles. They don't have the confidence in themselves to take on the leading role. Do you really want to be living your life in someone else's shoes? You can trip, stumble and fall on stage. You can forget your lines and get muddled. You can receive applause and standing ovations. It's all part of the journey, of learning and growing. The aim is to not be a one-hit wonder but to continually Make Your Mark. Many of us will not receive our star on the Hollywood Walk of Fame, but that's not the point. The point is that you can Make Your Mark in lots of little ways as you go about your days – and of course, in big ways too.

In order to Make Your Mark, at the intersection of clarity and connection is vision. This is where you know your big picture (your vision of the film you are staring in). It is where you take time to reflect on the journey (your scenes in the film). It is here that you reaffirm your "why" (what propels you forward when you forget your lines, and times get hard). It is where connection to self and to your audience is important, by showing up as your true self and knowing what you are doing and where you are going. It is where you get clear on the actionable steps required. It's choosing the soundtrack and anthem which empower you to shine your light bright. To Make Your Mark. You are a star!

YOUR MARK

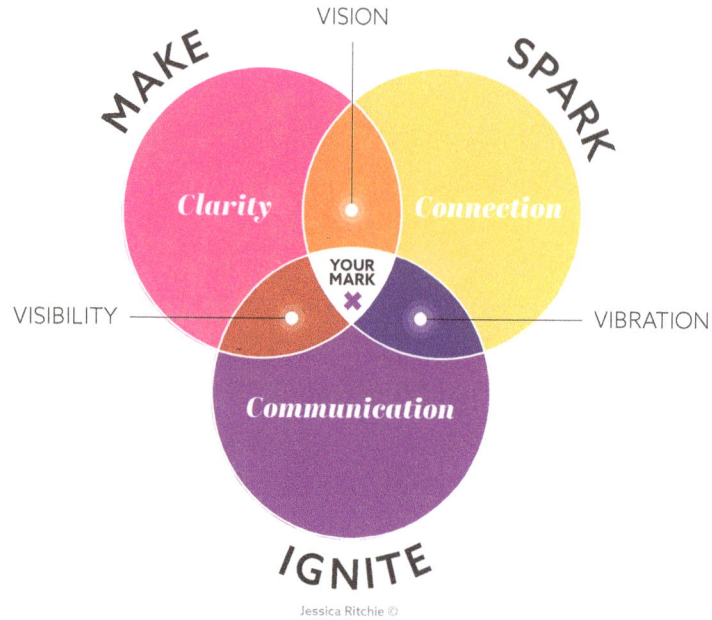

Has there ever been a time that you took a supporting role even though you wanted to be the lead role? I remember when I was in grade seven, I was itching to be the captain of the Red sports team. As a year level, we had to nominate and vote who we wanted to be our leader. It came down to me and my friend Alyce. I voted for Alyce, even though I wanted to vote for myself. I voted for my friend because I didn't want to look bold, showy and "up myself" by voting for myself. That one vote meant that Alyce became the captain, which put me in the support role. A lot of women naturally tend to do this. They take the back seat, the supporting role, the nurturer to someone else. You've probably heard the often-quoted "statistic" that women only apply for a job if they meet 100%

of the qualifications, whereas men will apply for a job even if they only meet 60%.[9] I don't believe that *all* women wait to apply for a job until they have 100% of the skills required, but I wouldn't be surprised if many women stop themselves from applying because there's only one or two skills they don't believe that they have. To smash the glass ceiling and to change culture and thought processes, you need to back yourself. You need to direct yourself. You need to support yourself. It's about showing up and declaring the skills, presence and essence that only you have to an opportunity. Acknowledging the skills that you don't think you have but noting *how* you will go about learning them. Having clarity and a crystal-clear vision will help you to do this.

Being the director means being the boss of you. Of owning your personal power.

Having a vision and being in the director's chair allows you to have more control over the controllables in life. Of course, we can't control the uncontrollable, but remember – the experiences that we deem negative, hard or challenging form the vital parts of the hero's journey in our own film. **Stars shine brightest on the darkest of nights.**

This is the benefit of having a vision: it allows you to be more proactive than reactive with your life. You can be more strategic, knowing you've got that vision to direct your work and life towards what you dream of.

---

9 Tara Sophia Mohr, "Why Women Don't Apply for Jobs Unless They're 100% Qualified," *Harvard Business Review*, 25 August, 2014, https://hbr.org/2014/08/why-women-dont-apply-for-jobs-unless-theyre-100-qualified.

Don't be afraid to hold the megaphone that comes with being a director; there's great power in using your voice. Learn your lines, get creative and curious with the script and be inspired by creating your own personal mantras (you'll learn how to do this in a few pages). Give yourself the elevated director's chair and utilise the heck out of the clapper board to cut/stop the film. You can have as many "takes" as you want. The most important thing you can do is to create and say, "And ACTION!" You can create as MANY films as you want, too, not just one. With each film, you'll get better and better.

You can always cease for a while to change the direction of your vision if you need to. You have permission to stop filming, to take time out to get the clarity required. You don't need to keep countless hours of tapes of material you don't want or can't use (like negative self-talk) rolling around in your mind. Let that crap go. Leave those reels that aren't for your best and highest good on the cutting room floor. They don't need to take up any more precious time in your film. Take them to the trash. Yes, I understand that these moments are still part of your story, but they don't have to be the ones that are highlighted or take centre stage. You have permission to direct as you see fit.

You have the power and the permission to lead yourself. You are the star of <u>your</u> story and it's incredibly exciting to see what you're going to create. Stop what doesn't feel right, even if it might not make sense to you (or others) at the time. Do what your heart is calling you to do, no matter how wild or out there it may seem.

Be the star; be the shining light in your own film. That's how you Make Your Mark.

Vision

Is it time for you to direct and lead your own story and get clear on your vision? I hope you're nodding yes because off we go to create your vision!

Vision is the "ability to think about or plan the future with imagination or wisdom."[10] To me, it also means giving yourself permission to DREAM BIG.

By dreaming big, you are creating a vision. How do you envision your dream? Your vision entails your purpose, your passion, your life mission and how you will Make Your Mark on a daily basis.

Your vision could be a world where you no longer dread Mondays and only live for Fridays. That would mean creating a professional life doing something you enjoy, which would mean you would love your overall life a lot more. Your vision might be to make money from your hobby, and blend your professional and personal lives more. Ask yourself – if you could do anything, be anything, what would that be?

If you don't know where you're going or don't have a vision for your future, I reckon it's a bit like catching a mystery flight. You have no idea where you are going, or how to prepare yourself. You might find yourself in Antarctica, in minus fifty degree weather without having packed thermals. Ain't nobody got time for that!

A **vision** is the bigger picture. **Your life's vision** defines who you want to be, what you want to be known for and the set of experiences and accomplishments you aim for. **Your**

---

10 *Lexico*, s.v. "Vision", accessed October 30, 2021, https://www.lexico.com/definition/vision.

vision helps define your goals by giving you a framework to evaluate those goals. Having a vision opens up a world where there are no bounds or constraints.

Personal Power Anthems

Each year I create for myself a **Personal Power Anthem (PPA)**, which helps me to reach my vision for the year. A PPA is a bit like PPE (personal protective equipment) – it's what protects your vision and your energy. It helps you understand what is required to achieve your goals and who it is you need to help you. Your PPA ensures that you keep on track and don't get distracted by "shiny object syndrome" (the tendency to be distracted by things that are fun or new but not necessarily going to get you closer to your dreams).

To create my PPA each year, I start with the help of just one or very few words. Those key words become the thread or the theme that I march (and dance) to for the year. I use them to keep my vision burning strong and my motivation high. If I feel distracted or not in alignment, I tune back into my key words that are the essence of my anthem. Identifying your key words also allows you to better understand which opportunities to say yes to, and which to say no to. It becomes easy to ask yourself, "Does this opportunity/person/event fit with my key word?" If it doesn't, say no and move on.

Jessica Ritchie ©

Now that you know your key words, and the theme for the year, you are able to choose a song that fits those words and embodies the energy you wish to harness in order to reach your vision. This is what creates your anthem. It can be any song, new or old, but choose a song that you can sing along and dance to. Yes, you read that correctly. Dance. Dancing to your song will help you raise your vibration, gain focus and propel you forward even more quickly to your vision. It will put a smile on your face and can get you out of a "funk" quick smart!

How to choose your key words/theme:

1. Sit down somewhere quiet and write down your goals. Nothing is out of reach, too big, too "out there", or too scary. Get in your director's chair and give yourself permission to dream big, be limitless!

2. What actions or steps do you need to undertake this year (no matter what date you start on) to fulfill these goals? Break your actions down into quarters, and then into months (you can even go down to weeks

and days once you have clarity on your goals). Be strategic about all your actions and how they will take you toward your goal. Don't just go with the fun, fluffy stuff (bright shiny objects).

3. What challenges might you face? What might stand in your way of reaching these goals?

4. Take a look at your goals, the actions required, and the challenges you've identified. Is there a common thread or theme running through them?

This process will help narrow down your **key word(s) or theme** for your Personal Power Anthem.

When I personally went through this process with my vision of writing this book, I knew fear and imposter syndrome could creep in. ("Who are you to write a book, Jess? Will anyone read it? Will anyone care? What if it is a waste of people's precious time?" Yep, I went through all the thoughts and emotions.) To reach my goal and overcome those challenges, I decided that I needed accountability, mini goals and timelines to give me a sense of achievement and to keep myself motivated; a dedicated space purely for writing; time marked out in my already busy schedule specifically for writing; and I wanted to always keep close to my heart WHY I was writing this book. I also knew that I needed to keep my health as a top priority with the additional workload that I was undertaking.

When I looked at my vision, my goals and the actionable steps required to reach it, the big words that came to mind were ACTION, FOCUS, DISCIPLINE, HEALTH, PRIORITY, and COMMITMENT. An element of TRUST also came into play.

For me, the standout key word that I decided on for my anthem this year was **FOCUS** (and it encompassed some of the other big words): to focus on writing my book, continuing to serve my clients, ensuring my family didn't fall away by the wayside in the process and keeping my health in check. Phew. I had the word "focus" saved on my phone screensaver and written on many post-it notes stuck around my office, my car, my computer, my bedside table and on the bathroom mirror as a regular visual reminder.

How to choose your PPA song:

After you've chosen your key words or theme, you can choose a song for your PPA – a literal anthem that embodies your key word. It can be any song, new or old, fast or slow, as long as it increases your energy and amplifies the results of your key words. This should be a song that you can march to the beat of at the times that you need help to stand tall in your power. It should be a song that makes you feel good, one that makes you want to sing and dance and achieve your goals.

To harness the word FOCUS, the song that brought me into the moment and propelled me forward was Imagine Dragons' "On Top of the World". One of the senses that came with my vision of how I'd feel once I'd finished writing my book was to *feel* like I'd conquered a mountain and was on top of the world. A Make Your Mark moment.

A friend of mine, Kathy Rees, who encouraged me no end to write this book, said, "You know, Jess, this book is going to be like birthing your third child." Geez, thanks, Kath … perhaps that was why I put the process off for so long! I do remember after having my babies feeling first, relieved; second, in awe and completely in love; and third, on top of the world. The vulnerability that comes with writing a book is like wearing your heart on your sleeve, which is also what happens when you become a parent. So, this song helped elevate me to focus, commit and harness that feeling that would come with ultimately achieving my vision.

A highly empathic client of mine, Mel, decided that her key word for the year was "release". Mel often felt weighed down; she took on other people's opinions easily and this was holding her back. Her anthem song was "Let It Go" from the Disney movie *Frozen*. She particularly loved the line, "Let it go, let it go, can't hold it back anymore." Mel changed the final "it" to "me" when she sang it, to personalise the anthem and give her sense of ownership. This allowed Mel to step into her personal power and achieve the vision she'd held dear for over three years.

You don't have to wait for the start of a new year to create your anthem. Start creating it NOW! And if you're a clever cookie and overachiever who has already aced their anthem for the year, go and create a new one! At times, I do a new anthem in ninety-day blocks, depending on my actionable steps towards my vision. Find what works for you and **your** vision.

I love helping people to develop their anthems and now I am going to walk you through how you are going to extend upon your vision even further. When I am working with my clients, I use my skills as a neurolinguistic programming practitioner to take them through certain visualisation exercises. This embeds their vision and we even "anchor" the Personal Power Anthem so that they can easily tap into the energy they wish to harness.

What is your Personal Power Anthem that is going to help get you to your vision this year? I want to see it and hear it!

Make Your Markercise

Anchoring Your PPA

Create your Personal Power Anthem using the steps outlined earlier and choose your song. Sit down with your eyes closed, and say your key words out loud while your song is playing. Imagine yourself achieving your goal and fulfilling your vision. When you reach that goal and vision, what do you:

- see?

- hear?

- feel?

- taste?

- smell?

Embody that vision, hold onto it and harness the energy of everything you imagine you'll experience when that vision is reached. Using your hand, physically press all that you've sensed onto a spot on your body that you can "tap" into when you feel the need to boost your vision.

You've now created it within your mind and potentially other dimensions, now it's time to bring it into reality in your life, and to Make Your Mark.

Vision Boards:

Creating a vision board that depicts your vision is another super powerful exercise and reminder to embody your vision. I'm sure you've heard the saying "A goal without a plan is just a wish." Live a life where you're purposeful every day. It allows for a life with fewer regrets.

1. What are the actionable steps required to get you to your goal and vision? What date do you want to achieve each of these steps by? What date do you want to achieve your overall vision?
2. Make a list of people who might help you achieve your vision.
3. Find images of or representing your vision, the actionable steps you need to take, and the people who will help you. These pictures might be of yourself, your team, your family, or your friends – anyone who you want to be in your vision.
4. Print these images out, and frame, laminate or pin them safely to a cork board so your vision board lasts. Display it with pride in a place where you will see it often throughout your day and inspire you.

There are some great apps that you can download for free to make this process quick and easy. I do find, though, that the "old-school" way of being mindful and intentionally finding images, cutting them out and gluing them onto a poster is incredibly powerful.

MAKE YOUR MARK
Mantras

Jessica Ritchie ©

Mantras are a great way to rewire and train your brain to accept your vision and the journey on which you are heading. I chose to use the word "mantra" for my work instead of "affirmation" because if I am honest, I love the alliteration of the m's! It sounds good so I am going with it! So to be clear, the terms "mantra" and "affirmation" are one and the same thing in the context in which they're being used here.

Mantras aren't just words you say, either out aloud or internally. To me, mantras are words that you speak with vigour and purpose from every cell of your being. Mantras become the energy that you strive to up-level to and become. Your mantra is your vision being voiced, and it is particularly powerful if you create your own statement that starts with the words I AM. By starting your own mantra with I AM tells yourself repeatedly that YOU ARE those positive words. That YOU ARE deserving. That YOU ARE owning it.

The mantra that I created to accompany my PPA when I was writing my book was, *"I am **focused** on creating actionable steps each day. I am disciplined, committed and trust that my vision will unfold as it should."*

Having gone through the above exercises and activities, now is the time to create your own mantras. I encourage you to create your own Make Your Mark Mantras specifically for you and your vision. Look at the key word or words that you used to identify your PPA. Use that key word to create your mantra. If you know what is holding you back, why you are procrastinating or not actively pursuing your dreams, write this into your mantra to give you confidence.

Keep your words positive. You don't want to be saying anything negative with conviction, it's high vibes and a positivity state only that you wish to embody! Below, I have shared some of my own that I've personally created to get you started. Use my mantras below to fuel your momentum and motivation to bring your vision to reality, to Make Your Mark.

Examples of Make Your Mark Mantras:

- ✘ "I am courageous. Every challenge is a lesson and with every lesson I am one step closer to my vision."
- ✘ "I am focused. Today I give myself a pat on the back for the focus I've attained."
- ✘ "I am powerful. I've got this. Now I shall go forth and achieve my vision."
- ✘ "I am successful. I deserve the life of my dreams."
- ✘ "I am grateful for this new day and the abundance of opportunities that it will bring."
- ✘ "I am ME. May I harness my unique gifts and present them to the world."
- ✘ "I am energetic. I have the courage to pursue my dreams with grace and vigour."
- ✘ "I am love. My future is full of love, joy and ease. I am in flow with my vision."

- "I am unique. Today I will showcase to the world the best version of me."
- "I am abundant. I attract success and positivity into my life with ease."
- "I am deserving. I trust that all is unfolding for my best and highest good."
- "I am going to do one thing today to get me closer to achieving my goals."
- "I am strong, I am determined, I am kind."
- "I am bold and brave. I can do this, I've got this. Now go and do it."
- "I am worthy. Today I will do something just for me."
- "I am a friend to myself. I give myself a pat on the back and a high five."
- "I am climbing mountains, conquering fears and embracing my vision."

Make Your Markercise

Make Your Mark Mantras:

Write down three mantras to propel you towards your vision to Make Your Mark. They can be as long or as short as you like. Read them out first thing in the morning, whenever you feel like you need some confidence or your attention is waning, and before you go to bed at night. You can also use them to set an intention for important meetings, events, or anything that is of importance to you, where you want to shift your state of being and feel confident that you're doing your best and giving it all you've got.

1.

2.

3.

Bravo! By embodying your key word, amplified by your Personal Power Anthem and Make Your Mark Mantras, you are elevating and amplifying your energy to move more quickly towards your vision.

MAKE YOUR MARK
Moment

When I started reminiscing about the story I am about to tell you, from way back when I was in high school, it really doesn't come as a surprise that I do what I do these days. Part of my business services is to create powerful brands, colour palettes, logos and content that amplifies the unique energy and essence of a brand, person or business.

I've always been passionate about teams and culture. When I was in grade eight, I was told that I was in Badila house. There were three other houses within the school – Triton, Orion and Pinda – which were all named after the different sugar cane varieties in our town, Mackay, which is located in central Queensland, Australia. I was devastated. No one wanted to be in Badila as it was known as "loserville". BADila. Badila was known to always place last in any event or competition. Classmates would laugh and make fun of students for being in Badila. What seemed to make matters worse, in my opinion, was that the mascot for Badila was a toad. A pest to Queensland (and other states), more popularly known as roadkill! The other houses had strong mascots such as a taipan, eagle and panther.

When I was fifteen, I was elected school captain and sports captain of Badila. I had belief in myself and what I was doing, and

I was excited to be a leader. It was time for me to sit in my director's chair. I had a vision of changing and directing the internal culture of Badila and how the house was perceived amongst my peers (and even the teachers). To do this, I had to change the anthem, the song that we were listening to and the story that we were telling ourselves. I created a petition to change the mascot. The toad did not have the same energy or hierarchy as the other mascots, and I wanted to even out the playing field. I wanted something we were proud of and that we voted on as a collective. Something that was OUR mascot.

I learnt that just because something has always been a particular way, or is a "tradition", it doesn't mean that it serves us for our best and highest good. The original house colours were brilliant. They were gold and purple. I retained these colours because they powerfully represented the values I wished to instil of loyalty, royalty, wisdom, and honour.

The resounding vote was for Badila to become the Badila Lions. In doing so, we elevated ourselves to King of the Jungle (or cane fields in this instance). My vision was to create a house that people were proud to be a part of. Rebranding with a lion reignited a spark and a vision that had been lost for years. I witnessed increased pride, loyalty, commitment, engagement, and performance. The mindset within the house changed as well as within the school. We didn't go from zero to hero overnight, but we certainly weren't "the losers" and coming last all the time.

By sharing my vision and creating the steps for it to come to life all started by having the courage to say, "This is not OK, we need a change." It enabled me to make my mark, to empower us as a collective and create an almighty team that marched to a new beat … to the sound of our own power anthem.

STEP 4

Unwrap Your Unique Gifts

"What makes you different or weird, that's your strength."

— MERYL STREEP

Did you know that you have a beautiful abundance of gifts within you? These are the things that allow you to shine, set you apart as your unique imprint on the world and create a positive impact on others. In essence, these are the intangible assets within you that help you to Make Your Mark. Your unique gifts are often what allow you to find your life purpose. When you know what you are good at, what it is that you enjoy, what makes you different and stand out, it creates clarity around your vision. Have you thought about what your gifts are?

I've found that it is a pretty simple question to ask, but it can be a tough question for some people to answer!

MAKE YOUR MARK
Moment

I remember when I was watching my then four-year-old son, Max, and twenty-one of his fellow peers graduate from kindergarten. All parents and caregivers were invited along for a special concert. We each sat in front of the makeshift stage in the classroom. There were luscious red velvet curtains to each side and a Christmas tree in the centre of the stage.

Max's teachers, Karen and Katie, announced that each child would walk down the middle of the room to the stage and place a gift under the tree. Karen then explained that, together, all twenty-two children had identified what each other's gift was, and so the gift that they each carried represented their internal gift.

When it was Max's turn, Karen announced to the audience that his special gift was in providing empowerment to others, that he often said, "To never, ever give up," and that he always encouraged others to do the same.

My first reaction was to cry with pride, the second was that I was so pleased that Max watching the DreamWorks movie *Turbo* (about *a* garden *snail* who dreams of being the greatest racer in the world and never gives up) over one hundred times had paid off. But on a serious note, I was so proud to know that my son empowered others and encouraged them daily to be persistent, to harness their resilience and to never give up. This I know for sure is a gift.

Some of the other gifts presented by Max's peers ranged from "making people laugh", "always including others", "making sure we are OK", "a great listener", and "good at story telling".

I believe that each of us has a special gift that we can offer the world. These gifts or talents are also considered our strengths. It got me thinking during the kindergarten event, "What is my gift?"

What Is My Gift?

If I had to narrow my gifts down to a list of three, they would be my intuition, empathy and my energy that assists me to make my mark.

Are you able to quickly and confidently say what one of your gifts is in just a few words? Many people struggle with this, and there are a few common reasons:

- ✗ It could be as simple as it never being a conscious thought before now.

- ✗ You might be aware that you would like to know, but just haven't taken the time to think about it.

- ✗ You've thought about it, but just aren't sure what your gift is.

- ✗ You hear people say what your gift is, but you don't quite believe it yourself.

> *"Hide not your talents, for they were made to be used. What's a sundial in the shade?"*
> — BENJAMIN FRANKLIN

If it is hard to think about your gifts, it might be easier to start with what your strengths are. If you know what your strengths are, this can then help to identify your unique gift.

For example, if one of your strengths is being able to communicate well, that might mean that your special gift is high levels of empathy. A high level of empathy is what might allow you to genuinely connect and build rapport quickly with others.

Gallup, an American analytics and advisory company, conducted research on people who utilise their strengths every day and how this affects their performance and overall life quality.[11] Their research found that people are six times more likely to be engaged with their jobs if they use their strengths every day.

The researchers also discovered that employees who were able to use their strengths more frequently experienced a plethora of positives such as:

- improved health and wellness

- less worry, stress, anger, sadness or physical pain

- boost to positive emotions

- increased energy to face the day

- higher engagement levels for tasks.

They also found out that building on employees' strengths was a far more effective way of improving performance than trying to improve employees' weaknesses. The data suggested

---

[11] Susan Sorenson, 'How Employees' Strengths Make Your Company Stronger,' *Gallup Business Journal*, last modified February 20, 2014, https://news.gallup.com/businessjournal/167462/employees-strengths-company-stronger.aspx.

that if a business encouraged their employees to learn their strengths, it increased individual productivity by 7.8%, and for teams that focused on collective strengths, productivity increased by 12.5%.

It really does make you wonder if you can you afford to *not* know the strengths and gifts of not only yourself, but also of your loved ones and those you work with.

If you are unsure how to discover your unique gifts, here's three ways to unwrap yours:

1. Take some **quiet time to do a self-reflection.**

    a. Write a short biography and description of yourself. Don't be self-conscious, just let yourself write. See if you are guided by your inner self to write particular words down. Look at the experiences or moments you included. Is there a theme or common thread?

    b. Write a list of ten things you are passionate about and good at now. Are there two or three common strengths that link these things?

    c. Write a list of ten things you enjoyed or were good at as a child. Remember those days before you felt the pressure to conform and be someone that you are not? Compare this list to the list of things you're good at now – what has changed? What has stayed the same?

d. Write a list of your wins and positive experiences – in business, in your career, and in your personal life. Reflect on big and small moments of success where you've made your mark. Can you identify the strengths that helped you when you felt that you were operating at your peak performance?

e. Write a list of challenging times you've been through, personally and professionally. What did you do well during these times? Did you receive any feedback during these experiences?

2. Ask people to help you do a **personal branding exercise**. Ask ten or more people you know – including family, friends, neighbours and colleagues – to describe you in three words, or share what they see as your three best strengths. It's a great (and relatively quick way) to discover what others value as your gifts. Compare the suggestions – are they similar descriptions, or quite different? Think about whether you agree with them or not, and why.

3. **Try new things** to discover different skills and passions that might just be lying within you! New experiences can really bring our strengths to the forefront.

I personally found it really handy to go back to testimonials and old emails that I've saved. I found a resounding theme of my three words in these, that allowed me to discover and amplify my unique gifts. (I will talk some more about having a special file of these Make Your Mark Moments in Step 6: Turn Imposter into Composer.)

I'd love to know what your **special gift** is and how this has provided or is going to provide you (know that you know!) the opportunity to Make Your Mark on a daily basis.

Here's to embracing the gifts that only you can give!

Make Your Markercise

These three Make Your Markercises explore the activities described in this step.

Self-Reflection Writing:

Put pen to paper and see if anything stands out.

- ✘ Write a short biography and description of yourself. See if you are guided by your inner self to write particular words down. Look at the experiences or moments you included. Is there a theme or common thread?
- ✘ Write a list of ten things you are passionate about and good at now. Are there two or three common strengths that link these things?
- ✘ Write a list of ten things you enjoyed or were good at as a child. Compare this list to the list of things you're good at now – what has changed? What has stayed the same?
- ✘ Write a list of your wins and positive experiences – in business, in your career, and in your personal life. Reflect on big and small moments of success where you've made your mark. Can you identify the strengths that helped you when you felt that you were operating at your peak performance?
- ✘ Write a list of challenging times you've been through, personally and professionally. What did you do well during these times? Did you receive any feedback during these experiences?

Personal Branding:

Ask ten (or more) people you know – including family, friends, neighbours and colleagues – to describe you in three words, or share what they see as your three best strengths.

Name	Three Words to Describe Me	My Three Best Strengths
1.		
2.		
3.		
4.		
5.		
6.		
7.		
8.		
9.		
10.		

Compare their suggestions – are there any similarities in their answers? Do you agree with their answers or not? Why?

_____

_____

_____

_____

Revealing Strengths Through New Activities:

New experiences can really bring our strengths to the forefront.

- ✘ Make a list of new activities you'd like to try, or new skills you'd like to learn.
- ✘ After you've tried any of these new activities or skills, write down your experience. Did you discover any new strengths? Did the activities confirm strengths you thought you had? Were you surprised by what you learnt?

STEP 5

Unshackle Your Fears

"She stood in the storm, and when the wind did not blow her away, she adjusted her sails."

— ELIZABETH EDWARDS

You consciously and unconsciously create shackles out of your fears that limit what you can achieve. It is breaking through the fear barrier that will allow you to move forward to Make Your Mark.

Often, I have found that what I am afraid or fearful of is what I need to do the most. As author Steven Pressfield wrote in his book *The War of Art*, "The more important a call or action is to our soul's evolution, the more resistance we will feel toward pursuing it."[12] Oprah Winfrey, in her book *The Path Made Clear*, recounted Pressfield's further explanation of this idea, that "no matter the dream, the shadow of resistance is inevitable. It's like yin and yang – you can't have the dream without shadow."[13]

What you need to do is have the courage to grab the key (which is doing the activity or "thing" that you are fearful of) and unlock yourself from your own shackles (your fears). By DOING the activity you can set yourself free. Sometimes you have to do it again and again ... and again.

When I fear something, that is when I find myself procrastinating. I do not want to do a particular activity, or there are times when I say no to an opportunity but I really want to say yes. These things that I tip toe around are what I **actually** need to do – be it personally or professionally – to elevate myself and to make my mark. I've discovered that when I overcome the resistance and fear that I feel towards doing these certain activities or taking certain opportunities, that I

---

[12] Steven Pressfield, *The War of Art: Break Through the Blocks and Win Your Creative Battles* (New York: Black Irish Entertainment, 2002), 12.

[13] Oprah Winfrey, *The Path Made Clear: Discovering Your Life's Direction and Purpose* (New York: Flatiron Books, 2019), chapter 4.

am propelled closer to my dreams and the life that I imagine. Have you ever felt that way?

Even Oprah has felt so nervous that she has had knee jerks from nerves and the feeling of an out of body experience. This happened when Tina Turner, the famous singer, invited Oprah to dance on stage with her.[14] Oprah, not feeling entirely comfortable to dance, realised she really had to just embody the experience and make the most of it. Oprah has commented that it was one of the best moments of her life, being on stage, dancing beside one of her idols and not caring if her performance wasn't perfect. What mattered was the joy that was felt and not feeling regret. Later, Maya Angelou, one of Oprah's mentors, sent her a song where she took note of the following line, "When you get the choice to sit it out or dance, I hope you dance."

Do you want to sit out the song of life due to fear? Or choose to dance anyway? I hope you choose to dance.

---

14 Oprah shared this story in her book *What I Know For Sure* (London: Pan Macmillan, 2014), 3-4.

MAKE YOUR MARK
Moment

When I was younger, I had such a fear of public speaking or even being in front of a crowd. I am not the only one – fear and anxiety around public speaking (known as glossophobia) affects up to 75% of the population. That is a staggering three out of every four people. I was one of them. I still can be at times, depending on the situation.

I remember once for a school play when I was very young, all I had to do was wave a picture of an elephant – I had no other lines or responsibilities, but that didn't matter. On the day of the play, I told my mum that I was sick to avoid having to do it. This avoidant behaviour continued for most of my primary school years, calling in sick for class presentations or when I had to speak at assembly. When I did eventually have to do it, my hands would be sweating and shaking and my knees buckling from nerves. Many times, I was so scared I thought I was going to pee my pants! That was until the fear of *actually* peeing my pants in front of my classmates became the greater fear over speaking. Once I realised this, it gave me the courage to step up and do the activity that I was fearful of. It was just like how elephants can be afraid of mice –something so comparatively small and tiny was having too big of an impact. I knew that I needed assistance. I asked my parents if I could have speech and drama lessons. They agreed, and with those classes, I flourished. I came to love the stage and performing before others. I was still nervous, with the sweaty palms and knocking knees, but I did it anyway because it became fun. The thrill of being on stage and the high of the adrenaline afterwards made me felt fantastic and I loved the pride that I had within myself for overcoming my fear. Overcoming this fear has led me to so many opportunities to be on stage speaking in front of people, hosting my own events, running workshops and seminars, presenting to large audiences. All of these moments I would have missed if I had let fear take over.

You can let fear have two meanings:

Forget Everything And Run
or
Face Everything And Rise.

The choice is yours.

When you focus on fear, worry, and doubts, you move yourself into a lower vibration. Energy goes where attention flows. If you move your focus onto the feeling of doing something anyway, despite fear, and concentrate on the pride that you would have within yourself once it is done, THAT is what attracts a higher energy and vibration. You need to *lean into feeling the fear* and doing it anyway.

"Don't let your fears overwhelm your desire. Let the barriers you face (and there will be barriers) be external, not internal."
— SHERYL SANDERS

Do We Need to Conquer Fear?

I don't think it's about conquering fear. To me it is all about awareness and acknowledgement. How to acknowledge and be aware of fear, how to give it space but not the authority or power to drown your dreams. Fear is there to protect us, to guide us, to make sure we are safe and secure. If you look at it from this perspective, rather than thinking you're always a scaredy-cat, then this will help. What is it that the fear is trying to protect you from? Identifying what you are fearful of assists in breaking down that fear barrier.

- Are you afraid of failure?
- Are you scared of looking stupid?
- Are you concerned that people won't like what you have to say?
- Are you worried that others won't like you?

Now ask yourself, what evidence do you have the fear is actually real? Ask yourself these questions:

- ***So what?*** So what *if* that happens?
- What is the likelihood of it actually occurring?
- What is the worse that could happen if it does?

Most of our fears are in our own head and never eventuate. But think instead of what really might happen *if* you do what you are fearful of. You will never look back and think to yourself, *What if I had just done that? What if I wasn't afraid?* You don't want to live your life with regrets. There is that saying, "I didn't regret the things I did, just the things that I didn't do." Make the list of what you didn't do in life as short as possible.

So ask yourself, "What if? What if I allow fear to take hold and stop me from doing this? What if I go ahead and do it, with my knees knocking, palms sweating and hands shaking? What if I did it? How would I feel afterwards? How will that move me closer to my dreams?"

The Greek philosopher Aristotle is noted as once saying, "He who overcomes his fears will be free." Sometimes it's not about overcoming fear, it's how to live with fear and allow it to sit beside you. You deserve to be like a bird soaring high and free from your self-imposed shackles towards your dreams.

MAKE YOUR MARK
Moment

I want to soar to great heights (metaphorically) in all areas of my life, so one day I decided to fly (physically). I took flying (OK, falling) from the sky literally. I knew in life that there will always be fears, so back in 2017 I decided to do one of the things that I feared most: sky diving. My sister-in-law Jade gifted me for my birthday the highest possible tandem jump at 15,000 feet. I wanted to show myself, if I can jump out of a plane strapped to a man that I don't know, there would be very few other activities that I would be scared of. And it worked. Every time I feel fear, I remind myself that I've jumped out of a plane at 15,000 feet, all while my husband and our children, Max and Billy, were watching me. I remember the elation and rush that I felt afterwards. My family were in awe (and relieved when I touched safely back to the ground). I remember Max exclaiming that he was so glad that my "balloon" didn't pop. I wanted to show my children we can do anything and try anything (within reason of course!). So, I use this experience when I don't want to do something that is, in actual fact, quite straightforward to do. Would I rather just pick up the phone and have this awkward conversation or go jump out of a plane again? Nine times out of ten it's not the latter. I'm sending you a challenge to find what might work for you! It's time to break through that fear barrier.

PPAs and Overcoming Fears

If you feel like you want a PPA (Personal Power Anthem) to help you to overcome your fears, then look no further than the wonderful song, "If I Were Brave", by multi-award-winning singer-songwriter, Jana Stanfield. Jana's songs have appeared on *Oprah*, *Entertainment Tonight*, the movie *8 Seconds* and more. I am deeply grateful to Jana for her permission to use the lyrics in my book. It is a wonderful PPA that you may choose to adopt as well once you've heard the wonderful song and read its lyrics. Here they are:

If I Were Brave

By Jana Stanfield/Jimmy Scott

What would I do if I knew that I could not fail?
If I believed would the wind always fill up my sail?
How far would I go, what could I achieve?
Trusting the hero in me.

If I were brave I'd walk the razor's edge,
Where fools and dreamers dare to tread.
Never lose faith, even when losing my way,
What step would I take today if I were brave?

What would I do today if I were brave?

What if we're all meant to do what we secretly dream?
What would you ask if you knew you could have anything?
Like the mighty oak sleeps in the heart of a seed,

Are there miracles in you and me.

If I were brave I'd walk the razor's edge,
Where fools and dreamers dare to tread.
Never lose faith, even when losing my way,
What step would I take today if I were brave?

What would I do today if I were brave?
If I refuse to listen to the voice of fear,
Would the voice of courage whisper in my ear?

If I were brave I'd walk the razor's edge,
Where fools and dreamers dare to tread.
Never lose faith, even when losing my way,
What step would I take today if I were brave?

What would I do today if I were brave?

To find out more about Jana, her music, her amazing voluntours and her charity which helps refugees to increase their skills and confidence, visit https://www.janastanfield.com.

I know when I first heard "If I Were Brave" I had goosebumps. I felt like I was ten foot tall and bullet proof! I had been procrastinating writing a presentation, and as I listened to the song it allowed the words to unfold and find flow. It helped me find my voice with courage and conviction, to shake off the shackles of fear.

Make Your Markercise

"What worries you, masters you."
— JOHN LOCKE

Unpack Your Fears:

It's important to identify *what* you are fearful of so that you can then start to shake off the shackles. It is about bringing your fear(s) into your conscious awareness so that you can then act. Take the time to unpack your fears. It often isn't an easy task, but it is worth it, I promise.

- Make a list of the fears you're conscious of. It doesn't matter if they're big fears or small fears, or if you think they might be a bit silly – just write them all down.
- If you think you are not consciously aware of all of your fears, ask yourself:
    - What do I shy away from doing?
    - What do I procrastinate about?
    - Are there conversations I should have with people, but avoid them?
    - Where did my conscious fears come from?
    - When did my fears cement into my being?

Make a list any new fears that these questions have raised for you.

Now, for each of your fears, work through the Unpack Your Fears Table to see how you can overcome your fears.

UNPACK YOUR *Fears* TABLE

My fears	How could my fear eventuate?	What would happen if my fear eventuated?
e.g. public speaking.	e.g. by being asked by a friend to speak at a wedding.	e.g. I would have to decide whether I would step up and do it, or sit it out and say no.

How would I feel if my fear eventuated?	What's the likelihood of my fear eventuating?	What is a positive outcome that could occur?
e.g. nervous and sick to my core, sweating, out of comfort zone.	e.g. 50% – I know my friend really wants me to speak at her wedding and might ask soon.	e.g. I will have done my friend proud, I would have spoken despite my fear, I would be proud of myself.

How can I reduce the fear?	How would I feel if I did something I was fearful of?	Once you've faced your fear, and perhaps even overcome it, how would that improve your life?
e.g. join Toastmasters, lots of practice in front of my dog, practice in front of a kind audience - my elderly neighbour, I can think of the regret that I'd have if I DIDN'T do it - watching someone else give the speech that I was asked to.	e.g. proud, glad it's done, excited to try it again, relieved, maybe even enjoy it.	e.g. I would feel more confident, I wouldn't regret not having the courage to be part of my friend's special day and make my mark with kind words that can last a lifetime and treasure special memories.

Jessica Ritchie ©

Now it's time to _shake off the fear shackles_ through utilising the following tips:

1. Imagine yourself doing the activity that you fear. See yourself doing it just as you want, successfully and without any stress or problems. Embody how good it feels that you've done that activity. Hold that feeling for as long as possible and embody it over and over again.
2. Know where you are going once you've conquered that fear. Keep your big vision and goals at the forefront of your mind to propel you forward and provide motivation.
3. Keep perspective. You could always be doing something much worse. Remind yourself that there's others who would much rather do this task than what they might have to do. (This is not to devalue or invalidate your feelings, but I find this reframing certainly helps me!)

4. Find someone who is good at what you have a fear of. Reach out to them to see if they are willing to have a chat with you, or engage them as a mentor or coach to help guide and support you. Ask them if they ever had the same fear and how they overcame it?
5. Identify the attributes and habits of those who do what you want to do. Try to develop those attributes in yourself. Start to include those habits into your daily routine.
6. Have a cheer squad and support crew who will keep you accountable to taking one small step at a time towards overcoming your fear. (You'll find more information on this in *Spark Your Mark*, the second book in the "Your Mark" series.)
7. Reward yourself when you do overcome your fear. Go out for a nice dinner, or buy that outfit you've been eyeing off. You deserve it!

> *"Most of us have two lives. The life we live and the unlived life within us. Between the two stands resistance."*
> — STEVEN PRESSFIELD

Which life will you choose? The sweaty palms and knees knocking and doing it anyway? Or to fear those mountains in the distance and never climb them? I hope that you don't choose the path of least resistance. I hope you choose the lived life, where you choose to dance and to Make Your Mark.

STEP 6

Beliefs and Belief

"Whether you think you can or think you can't, you're right."

— HENRY FORD

When I was in secondary high school, I considered myself a decent writer. I had always received A's in English when I was in primary and middle school (maths was a different story!). In high school, I was mostly receiving A or A- for my work, even B+ at times (which annoyed the heck out of me) – the A+ seemed elusive. I wasn't an A+ student, yet my work was being showcased to other students in the school as an exemplary model. It didn't make sense to me. I let my teachers know that my goal by the end of my final year at high school was to receive the highest mark that I could attain – an A+ on an assignment.

(You might be thinking, *What is wrong with a B+?*, and there's absolutely nothing wrong with being awarded a B+. I was a perfectionist and high achiever, sometimes to my own detriment, and I simply wanted to see if I could get top marks. It was a goal. A vision. Writing was my passion, something I enjoyed. It allowed my voice to come out confidently when, many a time, I didn't have that confidence to say it out loud in person.)

I told my teachers that I was committed and asked them to tell me or to show me how I could achieve my goal. I wanted to know and was hungry to apply the knowledge. A lot of the feedback that I received was vague. Fuelled by my mission, for my final assessment in my English class, I wrote and presented a piece on female genital mutilation (FGM) in Africa. In my opinion, it was strong, it was bold, and it took courage to talk about that type of subject as a female with 50% male peers in the room. I found a video at the local library that showcased women's stories to support my presentation. It pushed boundaries. And that was the point. I purposefully wanted to educate through shock factor. I received a rapturous applause from all of my classmates. I felt in my bones that it was deserving of an A+. I didn't get the A+.

Determined to seek out other opinions on my work, I submitted the same piece for an important final year exam. "Average at best" was the feedback. A few weeks later I was asked to represent the school in a Zonta Young Woman of the Year Award. I entered my FMG piece. The feedback was incredibly supportive and encouraging – and I won the award, much to my surprise, and from what I remember, the surprise of others.

The next year I went to university, where each subject required written assessment. For each of those I was shocked to receive the highest marks possible – high distinctions. I was awarded scholarships and academic merit certificates and special invitations to events. My faith in my ability was restored. I realised that other people's opinions are just that. Opinions. The only opinion that really mattered was my own. That I was pleased with my own work.

I am glad that I persisted and that I did not let my flame be squashed by the opinions or beliefs of others. The realisation that I didn't give up on my belief in myself and my ability was a relief. A relief that I didn't suck. That I was OK with my writing. But again, relief can be short lived if you're basing your worth on others! The relief can be removed with negative feedback from someone else within one second. This highlights the need to have strong self-worth and faith in your beliefs at all times. It will see you through the personal and professional knocks that you receive. Then it won't be so easy to dim your light.

What Are Beliefs?

A belief is an idea about the world that you consider to be true. Your beliefs can hold great power. Beliefs can work for you, or against you. It is up to you to decide whether they will alter your life positively to Make Your Mark or if they will extinguish your internal spark. Your beliefs establish the limits for what you think you can and can't achieve. They are the main building blocks of how you view yourself, others, and the world. They are part of your foundation.

Beliefs come about through your programming and are based in your unconscious mind. How you view the world and what type of lens that you see it through depends largely on your beliefs. Therefore, it is important to have the awareness to understand that things are only what you perceive to be true, as it is only your truth. The mind is extremely influential in that it will find ways to make what you believe come true, or at least make it seem that it is true.

Beliefs often come from your childhood and early experiences with those who were your main caretakers. It is through these experiences that you develop beliefs about who you are and where you sit in the world. This is why I choose to incorporate many stories of my childhood, particularly when I was at school, into this book. I want to show how the beliefs you developed in childhood can impact your adulthood without you realising or giving it much thought.

As so many of our beliefs are developed and established in our childhood, they become a significant, but unconscious, part of who we are. Beliefs are often so ingrained in us that we rarely question them, or their impact on our lives, as adults.

So how can you get visibility of your beliefs – what's shaping you, why you're making the decisions that you are – especially the ones that might be working to your detriment?

The Stories We Tell Ourselves

"A belief is a story that you tell yourself."
— TONY ROBBINS

We tell ourselves certain stories because it can be easier than facing the cold, hard truth. In those stories, we can find a kind of relief: If I believe *that*, then it's OK to display *this* kind of behaviour or have *this* thought. Those stories provide us with a sense of relief to know that the way we behave or think doesn't make us bad or indifferent. What are the stories that you are telling yourself? What are the stories that others have told you that have formed part of your beliefs? Do you know that these hold true?

Once you are aware of your beliefs, you need to be ready to face some cold, hard truths. Is fear getting in your way of doing things that you want to do, and you know that you can really do? Have you been telling yourself stories that you're too old, too young, too tall, too short, too attractive, not attractive enough, too thin, too overweight, not smart enough? That you have too many dependents, there are too many variables, that there's not enough money, or not enough time?

Find the excuse, reasoning or story that you're associating with that belief. Can you challenge that story? What will it take to remove or reframe the story and replace it with an empowering, more positive narrative? Is there any support or someone specific that you require to assist you?

> *"There are stories that we take on from our culture, and there are stories based on our own personal history. Some of those stories lock us in limiting beliefs and lead to suffering, and there are others that can move us toward freedom."*
> — TARA BRACH

Self-Limiting Beliefs

Beliefs that work to your detriment are self-limiting beliefs. Whether it is true or not, if you believe that you are limited within yourself in some way, shape or form, then that is what you believe to be true. Unfortunately, these self-limiting beliefs can then become true because you allow them to take hold and give them your power. The Dalai Lama once said, "If you believe you are too small to make a difference, try sleeping with a mosquito."

It's critical to your personal and professional success that you overcome your limiting beliefs so that you can achieve your full potential. To tread your own path, blazing your way to Make Your Mark for yourself, and for others.

> **Is it time to believe that you are deserving,**
> *of being worthy,*
> *that you can sparkle and shine,*
> *that you can Make Your Mark in the world and*
> *sparking and igniting shiny, glittery,*
> *inspiring fire everywhere you go?*
> — JESSICA RITCHIE

> *"If you accept a limiting belief, it*
> *will become truth for you."*
> — LOUISE HAY

How to change self-limiting beliefs

1. Awareness is key to understanding what you believe to be true.

2. Pay attention to your behaviour to find out what beliefs are not serving you.

3. Write down the limiting beliefs that you've held about yourself.

4. Change one belief at a time.

5. On a scale of one to ten ask yourself, "How much do I really believe this?"

6. What is stopping you from changing this belief?

7. What are the things or reasons that you know can disprove the belief?

8. What is the new belief that you now choose instead?

9. How is this change and new belief going to positively impact your life?

10. Write down the new belief so that it is visible for you.

11. Create a Make Your Mark Mantra (see p. 66) around the belief, for example: "I am deserving of going for this promotion. I know that I am great at what I do. I have plenty of experience and I know that I will be an asset to any organisation."

Have the courage to change your limiting beliefs to set a solid foundation to Make Your Mark. Some beliefs of mine that I realised that I could change when I identified them include:

- ✕ "I am too old to learn the guitar." I now have guitar lessons on my vision board, and a goal to learn at least ONE song on the guitar by the end of this year.

- ✖ "I'm not worthy of a loving, faithful partner." Before I met my Sam, I'd been cheated on in both of the serious relationships that I had ever had. Why would anyone else be any different? What was wrong with me that caused partners to cheat? I realised that it wasn't me at all, but I had to change my beliefs about my self-worth and what I deserved in a relationship. I stopped the limiting belief that my value and worth was based on anybody else.

- ✖ "I'm not good enough to have my own business." But then I saw how confident others who seemed less qualified were, including one person who admitted to reading a book on marketing and then starting their own marketing agency (yes, you read that right, they had no formal qualifications or experience yet they held the belief that they could do it). I thought, *Hot diggity damn, I NEED to be doing my work if there are people like this out there!* It sparked that need to be of service and to pioneer over profits at time in order to make my mark.

- ✖ "I will never have children." I listened and trusted several specialists who told me that for a decade. For years I held the belief that I couldn't have children. One day I decided that I could at least try and change elements of my health, even though specialists had said it couldn't be done. I was very lucky to be able to have children despite the health challenges that I faced.

✖ "People won't like what I say in this book." Every now and then, I still get this thought. Yes, imposter syndrome comes for a little visit. And then I remember, what has fuelled me to write this book is that many people have encouraged me to share my experiences and learning, and if my book helps just one person in one small way, that will make me a very happy person. My job will be done. I believe my thoughts have life and purpose, and I believe they will help people by being printed in one place, rather than hiding away in my pretty glittery stationery!

Take the time to be honest with yourself, what beliefs have held you back? Think about all the times you have limited yourself or changed your behaviour because of a self-limiting belief you hold. Then, think about **what it is that you are going to do now with this knowledge?**

MAKE YOUR MARK
Moment

When I was studying to become a practitioner of neurolinguistic programming, I discovered I held a belief that good people didn't charge a lot of money for their time, product, or services. I realised that this belief (like many of them) came from my childhood. It sparked memories of watching my dad, who is one of the nicest, kindest people that I know, help anyone that he could, no matter what. Dad is a mechanic by trade, so even if his own car wasn't running, he would go and fix other people's cars, even though he should have been prioritising fixing his own. It was like the old saying, "the cobbler's children have no shoes". Dad would never charge people for fixing their cars, it just wasn't in his nature. (I know there's also issues about boundaries and worth here, that's not the point of my story and I have had this chat with my dad!)

The penny dropped. I had learnt the belief that nice people didn't charge others money for a skill that they had. I removed that belief and instead instilled the belief that I could be a good person, help others AND charge what I was worth. I realised by charging my worth I could actually help a lot more people, and that I wouldn't end up doing it begrudgingly. That was a game changer for me that allows me to make my mark and elevates my self-worth, both personally and professionally.

I love this quote from Steve Jobs: "Your time is limited, so don't waste it living someone else's life. Don't be trapped by dogma – which is living with the results of other people's thinking. Don't let the noise of others' opinions drown out your own inner voice. And most important, have the courage to follow your heart and intuition." The quote reminds me that I need to know my own beliefs, and question those that I might have inherited from other people, and make sure that all my beliefs support *my* vision.

Is that a sigh of **relief** that I might be able to hear? Now do you understand that *it is possible* to change those programmed beliefs for you to take flight and to shine bright? Understanding your limiting beliefs allows you to gain further clarity: clarity to know who you are, to strengthen your mindset, to remove the beliefs that no longer serve you. To Make Your Mark wherever you choose to go.

Make Your Markercise

Breaking Down Detrimental Beliefs:

1. The beliefs that are not serving me are:

   ✗ _____
   ✗ _____
   ✗ _____
   ✗ _____
   ✗ _____

2. Identify which belief you are going to work on changing first.
3. Where do you think this belief came from?
4. How are you going to change this belief?
5. Commit to a date that you would like to change it by.

STEP 7

Turn Imposter into a Composer

"You wouldn't worry so much about what others think of you if you realised how seldom they do."

— ELEANOR ROOSEVELT

Have you ever had a visit from the imposter? You know, that feeling that you get as though you are about to be "caught out" or that you are not "good enough"? Imposter syndrome is the voice in your head that says, "You are a fraud! You should not be here in this position/doing this task/presenting this workshop/going for this job!"

Imposter syndrome is the feeling of inadequacy you might have about who you are or what you do, despite any evidence of success or achievement. People who experience imposter syndrome "suffer from chronic self-doubt and a sense of intellectual fraudulence that override any feelings of success or external proof of their competence."[15] A fear of failure and high level of perfectionism is also usually evident in those who experience imposter syndrome. Imposter syndrome often affects women, particularly when there is an expectation that they can do it all, or if they are the first or only woman to reach a particular professional position. Often there's fewer women in leading positions, which can sometimes mean there's fewer people to talk to who understand how high-achieving women feel.

Does this sound like you?

If you have felt this, then let me tell you that you're certainly not the only one. In fact, a 2020 study by the US branch of the multinational professional services network KPMG found that 75% of executive women reported having experienced imposter syndrome at times during their career.[16] More than

---

15 Gill Corkindale, "Overcoming Imposter Syndrome," *Harvard Business Review*, May 7, 2008, https://hbr.org/2008/05/overcoming-imposter-syndrome.

16 KPMG, *Advancing the Future of Women in Business: The 2020 KPMG Women's Leadership Summit Report* (2020 KPGM International Cooperative, 2020), https://womensleadership.kpmg.us/content/dam/womensleadership/pdf/2020/2020wlsstudy.pdf.

half of the women interviewed in this study (56%) feared that people around them would not believe they were as capable as they were expected to be.

The imposter might pay you a visit when:

- ✗ You are afraid that you won't live up to the expectations of yourself and others. (The imposter loves to visit those who are perfectionists.)

- ✗ You never thought you would achieve the level of success that you have, which contributes to a sense of self-doubt.

- ✗ You don't think you are deserving.

- ✗ You feel like maybe you're "just lucky".

- ✗ You dismiss praise.

- ✗ You think, "Why me?"

- ✗ You're afraid you will fail.

- ✗ You believe that you lack skills and talent.

Imposter syndrome hits even the most objectively successful of people. Maya Angelou, the American civil rights activist and highly acclaimed, award-winning author and poet, admitted that she often felt like a fraud, saying: "I have written eleven books, but each time I think, 'uh oh, they're going to find out now. I've run a game on everybody, and they're going to find me out.'"

I've felt imposter syndrome many times. Yes, I too have been down that wobbly path before and let me tell you, it does not serve you. It still comes and visits from time to time. Imposter syndrome speaks straight to your self-worth and allows self-doubt to creep in. If you cast your mind back to Step 2: Self-Worth, you'll remember from the Self-Worth Quadrant that listening to internal negative self-talk reduces our confidence by half. Imposter syndrome reduces confidence. It makes you second-guess yourself and can inhibit your communication if you listen to it. Imposter syndrome can take you off your path to making your mark!

Let me tell you about a time when I felt imposter syndrome come knocking hard and fast at me. I was just about to deliver my first Wondrous Women event (a networking series I established for women in business). I kept asking myself, "Why are there fifty women in the next room waiting to hear what I've got to say? Do I even have anything to say? Will they want to hear what I have to say? What if they don't like it and people just leave? Perhaps they think that I am someone else?"

Self-doubt was creeping in, BIG TIME! I needed to become the composer of my song and squash the imposter that was imposing on my day and my vibe.

I went to the bathroom to take a moment to pull myself together. Fear was talking alongside the imposter. I internally thanked them both for trying to protect me but admitted that they were not helping me so it was time for them to get out of the way. I said my Make Your Mark Mantra out loud, and I put my headphones on to listen to my Personal Power Anthem song for that year (Katy Perry's "Roar"). I literally shook out the nervousness that I was feeling through movement. I reminded myself that I was there to be of service and that I could do this. If anyone had peeked around the bathroom door, I am sure they would've thought I'd turned mad.

I turned the IMPOSTER into a COMPOSER. These tools allowed me to pull myself together. During and after the event, I received the most wonderful, heart-warming feedback about the positive impact that it had on many of the attendees. I have often thought about how the event may have gone if I had allowed the imposter to compose my song that evening. Instead, it became the first of many Wondrous Women events that enable me to make my mark.

When the imposter strikes, go back to your vision. I want to share with you a story about Ludwig Beethoven. This may be taking the whole "composer" theme too far, but here I go. I learnt the piano for several years and his works are still to this day some of my favourites. The Ninth Symphony is one of the most beautiful pieces of music ever written. The final movement of this symphony is the great "Ode to Joy" and it's now the European National Anthem. What's hard to fathom is that when Beethoven wrote the Ninth Symphony, he could not hear a single note of it. By that time, he was already profoundly deaf and in order to write the music he had to saw off the legs of his piano, place it on the floor and then literally listen to the vibrations through a glass held against his ear and the floor. His housekeepers also recalled seeing him put a pencil in his mouth and place the other end of it to the piano's soundboard to feel the vibration of the notes.[17] Beethoven tried to keep news of his deafness a secret from those closest to him. He feared his career would be ruined if anyone realised.

Beethoven had a vision and he was persistent. He couldn't hear his symphony, yet he composed it and brought it to life. When it was time to showcase his music, he went on stage and conducted it (with an assistant). Beethoven was so deaf, that he couldn't even hear the resplendent round of applause and standing ovation that the audience was sending his way. His assistant had to turn him around to see it. Beethoven envisioned all the pieces of his symphony without hearing it, yet he wrote it anyway.

Beethoven didn't let not being able to hear the world's best symphony ever created stop him from creating it. YOU can't let imposter syndrome stop you from creating your symphony and your life song. The Ninth Symphony is a powerful symbol of the grit and determination that it can take to Make Your Mark. It's time for you to write a remarkable symphony with your life, with the love and passion that you put into yourself, your work, your family – that you put into building your world. In doing so, you will make your passion and inspiration visible. Make the intangible tangible by creating your symphony.

---

17 "So If Beethoven Was Completely Deaf, How Did He Compose?" Composers, Classic FM, last modified 25 January, 2021, https://www.classicfm.com/composers/beethoven/guides/deaf-hearing-loss-composing/

How to Let Go of the Imposter and Welcome in the Composer

There are a few steps you can take if you want to challenge your imposter:

Awareness. Become aware of the times that you feel imposter syndrome rearing its ugly head. Is there a certain person or situation that triggers it? A reoccurring meeting? What are the words or feelings that you hear or sense when this happens? Write it down so that you can taking ownership of what's occurring and so you can also understand where it is coming from.

Give the voice of your imposter syndrome a name. Giving that pesky voice that threatens to weaken your disposition a name brings awareness and acknowledgement. It provides an identity which you can call out, like it was an annoying bully at school. I call mine Melody. I say, "Thanks for the melody, Melody, but I'm choosing to listen to a different tune that is positive. I am deserving of this position/award/interview/opportunity. It is time for you to go now. Goodbye."

Go back to your vision. Revisit your Personal Power Anthem to bring you back into your personal power. Say your power anthem out loud. Put on your song that accompanies your PPA. Have your anthem printed as a reminder and place it on your desk, wallet, car, fridge, mirror – wherever it is needed to remind you that "You've got this!" Take a look at your vision board and actionable steps. Most likely these steps need to be made to reach your vision which is why the imposter is rearing its head. Out with the imposter and in with the composer to achieve your dreams!

Revisit your unique gifts. Be sure to do the personal branding exercise in Step 4: Unique Gifts (see p. 84) of asking your colleagues, clients, network, friends, and loved ones for words that describe you. This will empower you and remind you of the attributes, essences and gifts that you bring to those around you. They are words in black and white that you can't dispute.

Look at it as a positive. Author and former business executive Seth Godin says that when experiencing imposter syndrome, we must embrace it as "proof we are innovating, leading, and creating."[18] Look at reframing the voice of imposter syndrome into a positive check-in, that it's just making sure you're OK and that you've got this. Turn the negative self-talk and doubt into a more positive mindset.

Remember you are human. Set *learning* goals instead of *achievement* goals. We all make mistakes. No one is perfect and how we learn is by making mistakes. Re-frame the situation if it is not a successful outcome. What were the learnings from this situation? What might you do differently next time?

---

18 Seth Godin, *The Practice: Shipping Creative Work* (New York: Portfolio, 2020).

Speak to someone you trust. Many high-performing individuals have a mentor, coach or an associate who provides them with guidance and support. Reach out to them and be honest with what you're experiencing. Chances are that they have also experienced imposter syndrome and may have some tips for what helps them.

MAKE YOUR MARK
Moment

Some years ago, I was asked to launch the business that I worked for at the time into the United States. One of the activities for this was a tradeshow at a world data expo in Las Vegas. Las Vegas, the mecca of tradeshows and events! I remember thinking, *How am I going to economically take a trade stand over to the States and create impact? How are we going to make a mark against the biggest players in the world and their equally big budgets?*

I'd done tradeshows many times before in Australia, but I allowed my mind to create this idea that I wouldn't be good enough for the United States. I had travelled across Australia numerous times to host events for large corporations to crowds of thousands. I'd created trade and exhibition stands for an ASX-listed company in Australian capital cities for premium mining and business industry events. Yet, I still thought, *Who am I to lead this and launch our business internationally?* All these thoughts came into play and were holding me back. I felt nauseous just thinking about it. I became aware that it was the imposter talking to me. Now being aware, I went through all the old testimonials that I'd received from prior workplaces, and looked at my photos of past trade stands to remind myself of my achievements. I remember thinking, *Well, who are you* not *to do* this? It's your job to do it, you're more than qualified to do it. It's a terrific opportunity. Fear turned into excitement. I composed myself and composed my tune to which I wanted to dance.

It turned out that the simplicity of the stand (which was necessary with the overseas travel restrictions and time limits), featuring just a few stand-out pieces of marketing collateral that I'd created, hit the mark. I had the organisers of the event as well as fellow exhibitors ask me to do assessments of their own stands. We even won an award for the best stand. Well, what do you know?

Moments like this are a reminder that we need to keep a rock-solid foundation of our identity and hold our vision close so that clarity is achieved. It's time to **be the composer, remove the imposter and Make Your Mark.**

STEP 8

Comparisonitis – Do You Dare to Compare?

> "A flower does not think of competing against the flower next to it. It just blooms."
>
> — ZEN SHIN

Have you ever compared yourself to someone else? It might be someone in your industry or workplace, another parent, or your sibling. Whoever it is, you place them on a winner's pedestal which in turn leaves you feeling like a loser who shouldn't even be running in the race.

I often have emerging high-performing female leaders reach out for assistance with comparisonitis – the compulsion to compare your achievements (or lack thereof) with those of others.

Let me tell you a story about Angela. Angela reached out to me with an SOS call when she was in her mid-twenties. She needed a sounding board to become clear on who she was and what her personal brand stood for. Angela was doubting herself and couldn't help but keep comparing herself to others in her industry, to another woman in particular. Angela identified that nearly all of her comparisonitis was triggered through social media. She would feel so flat and deflated after scrolling through her social media feeds.

It was a sure case of Angela suffering from comparisonitis. My motto when it comes to comparison is "Don't you DARE to COMPARE." Theodore Roosevelt summed it up perfectly when he said that "comparison is the thief of joy." I could certainly see that this was the case for this aspiring leader. Comparison was not allowing Angela to make her mark.

Angela was in such a state of paralysis and fear that she was considering changing the career that she loved. And that would have been a shame, because Angela's industry really needed her innovative thinking and her fresh energy. It would have been a terrible loss to see her give up on her vision because she was comparing herself to others. Angela said she was sick of feeling frustrated, of being sick in the tummy from the comparisons she was making, and her loss of confidence in her own abilities.

Comparisonitis can often occur when you are early in your career or just starting out in business. However, it can happen to anyone at any time. The key is to not allow it to take you off track and cause self-doubt – and in this case with Angela, it was also contributing to a lack of self-worth. **When you are comparing yourself to someone else, you are taking away much needed time and energy for creating *your* best self.**

I believe that we as human beings are hardwired (in some aspects) to compare ourselves to others. We use it for self-evaluation. It is like we need a tide mark to see how far we can rise, but we try and find that tide mark not within ourselves but in others; an external source that we consider valid. We then base our tide mark against another's mark to see how we fare. Well, that is not fair, is it? Someone else's tide may have risen at the crack of dawn, and yours is going to appear at midday. Perhaps your mark is not made daily but is a king tide that comes once or twice a year and blows everything else out of the water.

This is about YOU making YOUR mark against your own tide. Tides ebb and flow. They rise and they fall. That is natural. That is life. Continue to rise to your *own* level, in your own time. Make Your Mark.

> *"There's no comparison between the sun and the moon. They shine when it's their time."*
> — UNKNOWN

If you're feeling like you get yourself into a comparisonitis funk at times, here's some tips to get you out of it:

- Firstly, stop looking sideways – you will get a sore neck. If you want to look at someone, just look at yourself. Only compare yourself to who you were yesterday.

- Awareness is imperative. Knowing that you're in a state of comparisonitis is the key to the following steps. If you are not aware, you will continue to feel frustrated and unsure why you are feeling that way. For example, you might recognise that you feel sad or upset when you meet up with a certain group of people, but you hadn't realised that you'd been comparing yourself to them.

- Revisit your PPA! Rock out to your power anthem and preach your Make Your Mark Mantras to yourself!

- Take some time off social media. If you have to post regularly for your business, schedule your posts in advance so that you don't need to log on. The world will not fall apart if you're not on social media for a while. If you do need to stay engaged on social media, when you see something that triggers your comparisonitis, ask yourself, "Do I really know if what they are posting is true or valid?"

- ✖ Remember that everyone can feel comparisonitis at some point. Those that you're comparing yourself to may even be comparing themselves to you!

- ✖ Don't compare your start to someone else's middle. Don't look at their highlight reels. Just do you and stick to your own lane. When you stick to your own lane, and your own race, you're always the winner.

Like imposter syndrome, when you are aware of comparisonitis you need to start composing your own song and marching to the beat of your own drum. Don't try to compete with or dance to another's beat. It ain't right, and it ain't you. Stay in your own lane. Don't keep looking to your left or right – you will hurt your neck. Carve your own path. Own your own path. I dare you to do that.

Remember Angela, the client I told you about earlier? When she applied the above tips, particularly finding and using her PPA and her Make Your Mark Mantra each day, she found that her energy shifted and she was in a more positive mindset. Angela banned herself from looking at social media first thing in the morning and also later at night, she also "hid" the woman that she was comparing herself to in her feed so that she didn't keep going into a negative spiral. What Angela found was, that over time, she had built up her self-confidence and self-belief so much so that she won emerging female leader in her industry at an awards ceremony later that year. At that event, she encountered the woman she had been comparing herself to in person. Angela felt so empowered from her focus on personal development that she didn't compare herself to the woman at all (and she said it wasn't from just having won an award!). She said, "In fact, we are so completely different, that I can't believe I spent all that time comparing myself when I could have been fuelling my fire towards my dreams instead."

> *"She silently stepped out of the race that she never wanted to be in, found her own lane, and proceeded to win."*
> — UNKNOWN

MAKE YOUR MARK
Moment

A few years ago, I kept seeing Sarah, a woman in a similar industry to me, constantly appearing in my social media feed. Sarah always seemed to have time to create clever, eye-catching business content, consistently. It looked like she had time to wash her face, brush her teeth, put on a full face of makeup and ironed clothes, AND have her four kids ready and sparkling by 7 am each morning. I remember thinking, *Gosh, what does she have that I don't? How can she do all this every single day while I feel like I'm drowning?*

A few months later, Sarah and I finally met in person at an awards night, after she began waving frantically at me from across the room. Sarah gushed that she was "fan girling", she was so excited to meet me. I was confused. Sarah had never once liked, commented on or showed any sign of even seeing my social media posts. Yet, here she was reciting to me her favourite posts and telling me what she had gained from them. When I congratulated Sarah on her business and wonderful social media posts, she admitted that half the time the photos that she posted were taken the day before to make it appear as if she had her shit together every morning. She was also very brave and admitted that she was struggling with the constant pressure to create and "perform".

This experience held some big lessons for me and my comparisonitis. It really highlighted to me that I wasn't keeping things – especially what I saw on social media – in perspective, which muddied any clarity that I had. Being so focused on someone else was taking me further away from my goals and vision so that I was no longer in my director's chair of life.

Make Your Markercise

Comparisonitis Checklist:

1. Have you ever suffered from comparisonitis?
2. Is there a particular person or business that is currently causing you comparisonitis? Why?
3. How can you challenge your comparisonitis? What can help keep you focused on your vision?

STEP 9

Values – Your Guiding Lights

"Values will get you through hard times and good times. They are the things that give meaning and purpose to what you do."

— BARACK OBAMA

Values are what we deem to be important to us. They are like guiding lights for how we think, speak, and act – they guide all our behaviour on our life journey. Values are one of the powers available to you. They help you to get clarity and reach your vision with the right foundation blocks to Make Your Mark in your business, career and life. Some examples of values are loyalty, freedom, family, wealth, creativity, intelligence, wellness, security, justice and fun.

Values tend to be unconscious, and they are what motivates a person to aspire to be their best self and to fulfill their purpose. We also use values to consider judgement – was something good or bad? Or right or wrong? Values serve as a benchmark for how you live your life.

> *"A value is a way of being or believing that we hold most important. Living into our values means that we do more than profess our values, we practice them. We walk our talk – we are clear about what we believe and hold important, and we take care that our intentions, words, thoughts and behaviours align with those beliefs."*
> — BRENÉ BROWN

Why Are Values Important?

Values build your character and your identity. They are the very essence and foundation of who you are. Your personal values help you define what it is that you want out of life, what is important to you, what your priorities are and how you will go about fulfilling your potential. Knowing your values assists you in becoming happier and more fulfilled in all facets of your life. You use them as the guiding principles of your life. **Values are like a compass.** They become the coordinates to follow towards your vision. They help define your vision and mission. If you don't follow your values, you can get lost, and lose your direction to where you want to go. You might experience disastrous consequences if you don't follow values such as respect and honesty.

It is important to have a strong sense of self before you reflect and elicit your values. Why? If you do not know who you are, it can be difficult to pick the ten most important values for you from a list of many. It can lead to confusion a lot of the time because all of the values will sound nice and of importance. If you're clear on who you are – i.e., have a strong identity and strong sense of self – the more aligned your values will be to who you really are, on the way to becoming your best self.

> *"What lies behind us and what lies before us are tiny matters compared to what lies within us."*
> — HENRY STANLEY HASKINS

Where Do Values Come From?

Values are often created unconsciously and are a part of your identity. They allow you to discover who you are at your core, to understand the unique energy and essence within you at the very depths of your being. The source of your values is often family, friends, school, media, economic status, geography, church/religion. They can be discovered, challenged and re-evaluated through life experiences. Values hold a lot of power over how and why we do some of the things that we do.

The Difference Between Values and Core Values

To Make Your Mark both personally and professionally, you need to understand what your values are. Further to that, you need to discover the solid, unshakeable values you have – in other words, your CORE values. These core values are not negotiable or moveable for you. Above all else, you require these values to be met, otherwise you will feel as though you are not living congruently; you will feel out of alignment, frustration will creep in, and you will have the sense that something is missing. Values such as safety, respect, happiness, and trust are generally a given – they are what we all want and so I tend not to include them as a key focus when eliciting core values. Try and dig deeper, past "the usual" to understand what really drives you and makes you tick.

My core values are justice, family, empathy, connection, and authenticity. These are my requirements to *function* effectively. These values are something that I *just couldn't* let go of and would have to continue to meet despite all else, otherwise I would be feeling incongruent and misaligned. My top values that extend outside of my core values are generosity, wealth, kindness and self-care. I can live *without* these values being met, even though they are important to me. It means if I had to, my priority for them can drop down what I call my "value priority ladder", if required.

Needs That Are Amongst Values

Needs are often what you focus on in the present, what's going on for you right now in this moment. Values are the more consistent driving forces that you have to reach certain states or goals. Some basic emotional needs that most people require include:

- being safe

- feeling secure

- being loved.

I think it's safe to say that the majority of people in the world need a sense of safety, security and love. They are fundamental needs. Sometimes needs and values can be the same, but not often. For a need to also be a value depends on the depth of the need and the space that it takes within one's life. A good example to showcase the difference between security being a need or a value is with my husband Sam. For him, security is a need but it is also a core value of his, as he lives and breathes it in his daily work as a police officer. He also volunteered at the non-profit organisation Drug ARM for many years in his spare time too, where he worked to give individuals and families experiencing addiction a sense of security. You can see that if you are on a mission to meet people's need for security, within your occupation or by volunteering, it can also be a value or core value.

Do Values Change When Your Life Changes?

When you reach certain stages in life, develop greater responsibilities, or go through a significant change or experience, you may feel pushed (either consciously or unconsciously) to re-evaluate your values. Your core values, more often than not, will stay the same despite the many changes that can occur in your life. Your values may change from time to time, although if you know what they are and you are living congruently they really shouldn't change too often.

An example of a complete values overhaul is showcased in the international best-selling book *The Monk Who Sold His Ferrari* by Robin Sharma. The book is about a fictional character named Julian Mantle. Julian is a high-performing and highly coveted lawyer who from the outside has "made it" in life. However, his health is suffering due to the stress and pressure of his career and the lifestyle that he lives. Julian decides to leave his career and incredibly wealthy life behind, to live with the bare minimum and seek solace in the Himalayan Mountains. There he finds peace and takes the time to reassess his values. His core values had changed, no longer focusing on wealth and status. He could now view how they could be used for the greater good and not for individual gain. Through his contemplation of the meaning of life and discovering how to not lose sight of what matters most for what matters least, he completely transforms his life mentally, physically, emotionally and spiritually.

Your values may not need such an extreme overhaul as Julian Mantle's did. What I believe can or does change for most people is their **value priority ladder.** What *priority* do you place on those values at this point in your life due to life changes? This is why it's important to know your values so that you can hold them close through both the good and bad times in life to make the best choices at that time. Values are like coordinates on a map to use your compass to guide you well on your journey.

My value priority ladder was out of whack for me prior to my husband Sam's work incident (shared earlier in Step 1). A value (not a core value) that was high on my priority ladder was wealth. I was spending an enormous amount of time working, which meant extended periods of very late nights and early mornings spent at my desk. This took me away from spending quality time with my family. The experience of fearing that my husband was never coming home taught me that while building wealth and being financially secure was important to me, it wasn't as important as finding connection with my family and spending quality time together. Connection moved up my value priority ladder while wealth (while still important) moved down. When our circumstances change, so too can our values if the circumstances alter our perspective on what's important.

Values and Goal Setting

It's important to allow yourself, your loved ones, and your team or workplace to explore values to assist in goal setting. By doing this you can come to understand what is critical for yourself and others in their life. When you know what your values are, you know what intrinsic need is driving you, and that provides **clarity** around what you really want in your business, your career and in your life. Once you know your values, you can then understand and identify how they align with the values of your family, friends, workplace, business, and clients. In fact, values are within everything that you do, every interaction that you experience, and in every thought that you have.

Values are critical to how you grow and develop. Understanding your values allows you to discover what is important to you. When you know and understand your values, it helps to drive you towards your goals with more focus and allows you to live congruently and authentically.

Values assist you in making deliberate choices to achieve your goal of creating the life you want to experience. Your values form an integral part of your decision-making process hundreds of times per day. In order to achieve what it is that you want personally and professionally, you need to discover what your values are so that you can be strategic in your decision-making to propel you further towards (and more quickly) to your goals.

By understanding your values, you can say yes to the right things, people, and opportunities more quickly, and you will have the power to say no to others with more confidence because you know where you are wanting to go, using your core values as a key piece of your foundation. From a professional perspective, when values are communicated and shared effectively within an organisation, it enhances culture and cohesiveness. When values are communicated externally, it helps to build trust and attracts clients and customers who are aligned with your values to your organisation.

Importance of Values for Brands and Workplaces

Brands and workplaces will look to values when creating their mission and vision statements as well as during the onboarding of team members. Values underpin and drive organisations, creating the culture required to achieve their mission and vision. An organisation might look for values such as respect, compassion, honest, loyalty and creativity to enhance their mission and the experience that is provided to both their team and also to their customers and clients.

It's important for you to understand your values *before* you work for an organisation. When you know your values and core values, you can find out if they will align with the workplace in which you are looking to work. Having your values align with your professional environment greatly assists with increasing your work contentment and feeling like you're making a positive impact in your industry. You can Make Your Mark.

From a business and career perspective, values can make or break your success. In my opinion, in many organisations, values are not communicated clearly enough to team members to bring them along with the organisation's vision and journey from the very beginning. Even if they are communicated early, they aren't revisited often enough. Some workplaces don't even know their values or worse, just don't adhere to them and lack complete congruence between what they say and then what they do When it comes to leadership, I believe that it is your values that determine your team's respect, productivity, performance and loyalty. When your values are weaved throughout all that you do, your way of living and doing work, all decisions will be made with those values at the core of your actions. This is what helps to build congruence and alignment (again both personally and professionally) in your personal and business brand, which helps you to reach your goals and ultimately drive your success.

The careful integration of values with strategy, mission, and goals also has a direct and measurable impact on customer retention, scalability and profit. One study found that 64% of consumers cite shared values as the central reason they have a relationship with a brand,[19] while another study found that brands with a high sense of purpose saw an increase of 175% in the monetary worth of their brand over a twelve-year period, well above the 86% median growth rate.[20]

---

19 Karen Freeman, Patrick Spenner, and Anna Bird, "Three Myths About What Customers Want," *Harvard Business Review*, May 23, 2012, https://hbr.org/2012/05/three-myths-about-customer-eng.

20 Kantar Constulting, *Purpose 2020: Inspiring Purpose-Led Growth,* https://consulting.kantar.com/wp-content/uploads/2019/06/Purpose-2020-PDF-Presentation.pdf

Now more than ever, according to leadership strategy expert Brent Gleeson, people want to buy products and services from companies that "have a purpose that resonates with their values and belief systems. They will even go out of their way to avoid companies that don't mesh with what they believe – which goes to show that a company's values have both internal and external implications."[21]

---

21 Brett Gleeson, "Why Core Values Matter (And How to Get Your Team Excited About Them)," *Forbes*, March 30, 2021, https://www.forbes.com/sites/brentgleeson/2021/03/30/why-core-values-matter-and-how-to-get-your-team-excited-about-them.

Make Your Markercise

So, you're probably thinking, *OK, I understand I need to get clarity around my core values and values. How do I do it?* While there are a few different ways that you can discover your values and core values, I have found two exercises particularly useful.

The Values List

This is a way to gain a quick understanding of your values. Look at this list of values. This list is not exhaustive; however, it is comprehensive enough to assist you in eliciting your values.

Achievement	Curiosity	Leadership	Responsibility
Adventure	Determination	Learning	Security
Authenticity	Diversity	Love	Self-Care
Authority	Fairness	Loyalty	Self-Respect
Autonomy	Faith	Meaningful Work	Service
Balance	Fame	Openness	Spirituality
Beauty	Family	Optimism	Stability
Boldness	Friendships	Patience	Status
Challenge	Fun	Peace	Success
Citizenship	Growth	Pleasure	Trustworthiness
Community	Home	Poise	Vulnerability
Compassion	Honesty	Popularity	Wealth
Competency	Humour	Recognition	Wellbeing
Compliance	Influence	Religion	Wholeheartedness
Contribution	Inner Harmony	Reputation	Wisdom
Creativity	Knowledge	Respect	

Choose no more than ten or twelve values from the list that resonate with you and that you value most in your life. We might resonate with all these values in some way, but it's important to identify which ones are the most important to you. Once you have made your shortlist of values, ask yourself these questions:

- Which of these values would not be negotiable for me to live a purposeful, aligned life?

- What are the values that make my life better?

- What values not on my list do I want to have?

These are the key drivers to what you do and why you do it. They are the very essence and core of what makes you who you are. **These are your core values.**

I like to limit core values to no more than five. This makes it easier for you to recall and hold them close so that you can keep aligned and congruent, which makes for fast and effective decision-making. From a metaphorical perspective, it also means that "you've got your whole world in your hand", with each finger representing a core value.

The Wheel of Life:

Another option, which is more in-depth, is using the **Wheel of Life**. The Wheel of Life is a simple but powerful tool that can help you see all the important areas of your life, all in one place. By showing you a visual image of all the parts of your life at once, the wheel helps you to take the time to discover your values for each element in your life.

What I find is that most people's values will be very similar, if not the same, across all the elements of their life. However, this is a good exercise to reflect on each facet of your life, identify your values and see which facets in your life may need some extra time or attention to assist you to Make Your Mark.

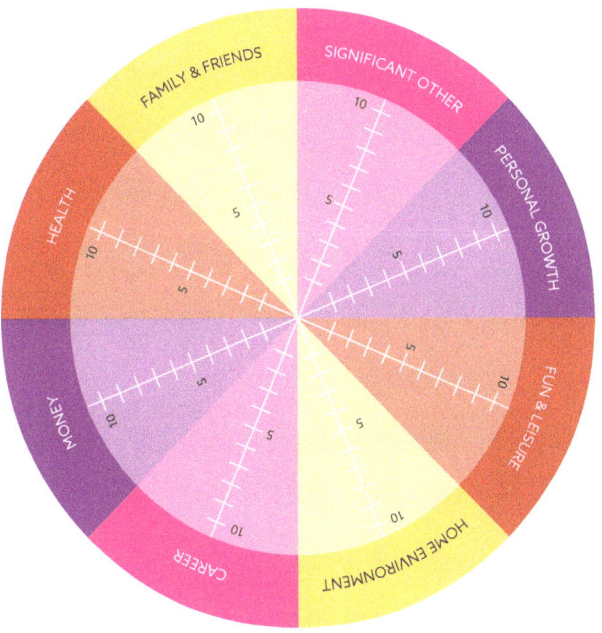

Jessica Ritchie ©

Choose an area in your life from the Wheel of Life. For that area, ask yourself, "What is important to me about this area?" and note your answers. Keep asking yourself "What else is important?" until you elicit six values.

Once you have your list of the six most important elements for you in that particular area, order them from most to least important.

Example: Values for the Personal Growth segment might be:
1. Fun
2. Growth
3. Freedom
4. Curiosity
5. Wisdom
6. Determination

Once you have your six values listed, now ask yourself the question, "Out of ten, with ten being 'fully met' and zero being 'not met at all', how well is this value being met in my life right now?"

Example:

BEING MET	VALUES	BEING MET	VALUES
4	Fun	8	Curiosity
9	Growth	8	Wisdom
5	Freedom	9	Determination

Any value that you rate as being seven or under on the "being met" scale is a value that has room for improvement. A rating above seven means the value is being met almost all of the time. A rating of seven indicates that the value is performing well but there is still room for improvement. A rating between five and seven shows that the value is being met some of the time, and any value rated under five needs time and attention to enhance its being met. Further probing and questioning is required to determine why you might have values with a rating of seven or below:

1. What is important to you about that value regarding that area of your life?
2. What can you **continue** to be/do/have in order to get those values met?
3. What can you **start** to do/be/have in order to get those values met?
4. What can you **change** in order to get those values met?

Now move onto *another* segment of the Wheel of Life to determine your six values for that area in your life. Once you have done each segment, go through and identify any reoccurring values. Narrow these down to no more than five. **These are your core values.**

Now that you are aware of your values and core values, this will provide you with clarity and confidence, aiding in your decision-making and goal setting, and allowing you to live a more aligned and congruent personal and professional life. You now know what it is that you are adhering to. If you refer to your values constantly (just like you would refer to a compass if you know the coordinates of your destination), you will be a lot less likely to get lost, and more likely to increase your chance of making your mark. This in-depth exercise will also help you identify which facet(s) of your life might require some extra time or attention in order to bring more overall balance and alignment to your life.

MAKE YOUR MARK
Moment

"Values are like a magnet; they attract good people."
— JOHN WOODEN

When I reflect on my professional career, I can say hand on heart that I am grateful for the amazing brands and people that I have worked with. What I wish that I knew sooner, which may have prepared me for some of the environments and people I worked with, was the importance of taking the time to get absolutely clear on my values and core values. I now have a business that is firmly based on my values, which attracts clients and opportunities with similar values – and this produces what I feel is like magic! The work we do is fun, it's creative, and it's all delivered and worked within a kind and empathetic environment.

I'm often asked to speak on the importance of identity and knowing your values in both your personal and business brand. Knowing who you are and what you stand for with your values can be the difference between making and breaking yourself, both personally and professionally. There is one moment that I went through that really showcased this for me.

For a long time, I didn't talk about or share my experiences of the terrible 2010-2011 Queensland floods. A series of catastrophic floods hit the state, leaving over thirty people dead, thousands of people homeless, and many others without businesses and livelihoods.

In the very early hours on the 12th of January, 2011, I woke with a feeling of dread and feeling physically sick. Over the previous few days, I'd watched the news in horror at the devastation and loss of life experienced in Toowoomba and the Lockyer Valley as floods swept through the region. I was living in an inner-city suburb of Brisbane, which I couldn't be sure was a disaster-proof area, so my gut was telling me that I needed to stay home that day in case of flooding.

Trying to listen to that gut instinct, I called my boss and asked for permission to work from home that day as I lived a minimum of forty-five minutes by car from my workplace with multiple rivers that needed to be crossed. My request was denied. I was told that they were going about their day as per usual, and I was to as well. I didn't want to rock the boat, so, unhappily, I went off to work as normal.

I was in meetings all morning, not knowing what was unfolding outside. My (now) sister-in-law Jade called me to say that an immediate evacuation warning had been announced for my suburb. My mindset shifted. I told my boss that I was leaving to prepare my home as per the evacuation order no matter what, and off I went.

I managed to get home in time to place some belongings high in a cupboard, and pack a few essentials in a backpack. By the time I had done this, which was just a few minutes, my garage had been inundated by half a metre of water. I knew I had to leave quickly to ensure my safety. With only my backpack, I waded out of my apartment through the icy waters, down the street, under a train crossing, and up to higher ground.

It was at that point that I realised I had nowhere to go. With many roads blocked off or underwater and a city in gridlock with other people trying to evacuate, I was unable to get to friends' houses or even the evacuation centre. I decided to surrender, trust and just allow the path to unfold, as I took (or waded) one step at a time. Two of my values are kindness and empathy, but I realised just how important these values were to me when a four-wheel drive full of Irish backpackers – complete strangers, facing a natural disaster in a foreign country – picked me up, and took me back to their place for a warm shower, a change of clean clothes, to charge my phone and have a warm cup of tea. I call them my "Irish Angels".

Over the next few days, I learnt that the lower level of my apartment building had been entirely flooded, and the water had risen high enough to flood the second level as well. As the water eventually subsided and I was able to gain access to the apartment, I remember thinking, *Where do I even start with the clean-up?* It seemed impossible.

I was so numb, in absolute shock. I couldn't think or feel. But this was when I saw the best in people. "Mud Army" volunteers were my saviours; no task was beneath any of them, no matter their stature in the community. They embodied the value of empathy, scraping sewerage-filled mud off my walls. A man who was integral in developing IVF technology in Australia was by my side, helping me sort and throw out my ruined belongings. In this instance, a quote from Albert Einstein kept coming to my mind: "Try not to become a man of success, but rather try to become a man of value." These were truly people who knew their values, and lived by them.

I recall the fresh scones, hot cups of tea, bottles of water, and barbequed food that were delivered by complete strangers as we all worked to clean up. My muddy ironing board was the table upon which we had our communal gatherings. These people were a shining light and a beacon of hope in what felt like my darkest hours.

But through all the months of cleaning up, re-establishing and renovating my destroyed home, I had to continue to work – and for the same boss who hadn't let me stay home that fateful morning of the flood. For me, this was the final experience that really made me aware that my values were not being met in the career segment of my life. My values had been tested by the lack of empathy and kindness that my boss had shown to me. This person had previously called me a bitch multiple times in a meeting in front of other colleagues (apparently as a term of endearment), restricted my learning development opportunities as "punishment" for my standing up for myself, and purposefully rewarded other people for work that I had achieved. I felt disheartened because the organisation's values were aligned with mine, but the values of the person who held power over me in that organisation clearly were not.

I decided that after experiencing all of this, I could no longer work for that organisation. We all have a right to security: having a safe place to live, and a safe place to work, and I felt like I had lost both of those.

My experience also made me realise that intuition (my gut was right from the time I woke that morning) is pivotal in ensuring that we are being aligned with our values and holding firm in what we feel is right. If you don't, you can lose everything – sometimes literally, like I did. It was such a big lesson for me in really knowing my values, what they mean to me, how it can impact me when I go against them or have them compromised by others and to hold them dear.

When you've lost everything, you don't care so much anymore about what can go wrong, only what can go right. I have learnt to live by my values at all times, listen to my intuition and gut – because if you don't, you can lose so much, and not just material items. It's about having the courage to use your voice when your values feel compromised, to do what is right for you. I wish I had acted sooner despite being told not to. Never again (fingers crossed).

> *"Open your arms to change but don't let go of your values."*
> — DALAI LAMA

STEP 10

Intuition – Finding Your Inner Guru

> *"You've always had the power, my dear, you've just had to learn it for yourself."*
>
> — GLINDA THE GOOD WITCH,
> THE WIZARD OF OZ

You already have everything that you need inside you to Make Your Mark. Yes, you really do. And there's one particular superpower that I find is often underutilised: your intuition. Or as I like to call it, **your inner guru.**

Your intuition provides whispers of warning or whispers of wonder. Do you ever hear or feel the whispers? Those thoughts or feelings that alert you to something that you should be doing, or something that you could change? Your intuition can be a wonderful tool for guidance and support if you so choose.

Intuition is the "ability to understand or know something without needing to think about it or use reason to discover it, or a feeling that shows this ability."[22]

> *"A gut feeling is actually every cell in your body making a decision."*
> — DEEPAK CHOPRA

For me, intuition is my internal compass, gut feeling, instinct, the whispers and taps on the shoulder that come my way ... the inner guru that is just waiting to be listened to. Intuition is like a lighthouse. It can navigate you through choppy and uncharted waters. It is the beacon of safety that guides you home or to the destination you wish to reach. It is where you can be safe and secure in the knowledge that you've made the right decision.

---

[22] *Cambridge Dictionary*, s.v. "Intuition," accessed October 30, 2021, https://dictionary.cambridge.org/dictionary/english/intuition

To Make Your Mark you need to harness the superpower that is your intuition.

Have you ever had that feeling in your stomach, like something is not quite right? Have you then gone against those feelings and ended up in a situation that wasn't nice? You think to yourself, *I KNEW that would happen. Why did I not listen?* In my experience if it does not "feel" right, then it usually isn't.

Conversely, have you ever had your entire body tingling with excitement at the prospect of something, just feeling that it is right thing to do? I sometimes get this feeling before entering a raffle I end up winning, or when I get inspiration for a new idea that turns out to be great. I feel giddy and spine-tingly! If you tune into these feelings, it will help you to Make Your Mark more frequently. I love this quote from the thirteenth-century poet, Rumi: "There is a voice that doesn't use words. Listen."

I've had friends say that they knew that they shouldn't have married their spouse, that they felt deep down it wasn't right but hoped things would change once they were married. I have had feelings to take a detour when driving only to find out later that my usual path had had a bad traffic crash, and I would have been delayed hours. I have cheekily messaged pregnant friends to say, "When are you going to tell me you have had your beautiful baby?!" For some reason, I just know – they get a laugh out of it and often shake their heads in disbelief.

Maintaining a Sense of Control

There are the moments and situations in life that, despite your intuition, you cannot control. I knew that something was going to go dreadfully wrong in the weeks leading up to that day my husband Sam went to work, the day that another police officer lost his life. For weeks before, I constantly had hiccups because I wasn't breathing properly, which is always my BIGGEST sign that something is up and I need to take note and listen. I realised that I was taking mental snapshots of Sam every day before he went to work, as I watched him walk out of the house to the gate. I told myself I was crazy. I felt crazy for doing it, but I could not stop it. When the situation was unfolding, I no longer felt crazy – I had known. If I needed "proof" that my intuition was, in a way, a gift, then I had all the proof I needed.

I had another occurrence of the hiccups when I was travelling through Thailand. I just knew that I had to get back to my resort. I arrived just in time to receive a phone call from my mum. She had been admitted into hospital for life-saving surgery. Thankfully, I got to speak to her before she went in. Another time I recall experiencing extreme edginess and hiccups was days before my brother was paralysed. The unease was palpable and all I could do was pray. I didn't know who it was about, or what or when something would happen, I just knew that it would. I have had many other experiences like this.

If you are highly intuitive and you can feel a situation brewing, that feeling that something is going to happen, you need to listen and act upon it. Doing something and acting upon your intuition can provide you with a sense of peace or comfort. For example, when I was in Thailand and I got the call about my mum going into surgery, if I hadn't followed my intuition and didn't get back to the resort in time to speak with her, and the surgery *hadn't* been the success that it was, I would have found it very difficult to live with that. You must do whatever it is that you believe will help protect you and whoever needs assistance. After that, you need to believe and trust that you have done all that you can. There's only so much that we can do; we are only human. The rest will unfold as it should, as hard as this is to accept at times.

I want to talk about using your intuition for the times **where you can** have certain control over situations. Generally, it is when we are going about our everyday life that we are able to maintain a sense of control through using our intuition. Recently, one of my team members shared a story with me about *not* following her intuition. As she parked her car at the shops, she thought, *Hmm, I don't know about this parking spot, the other car is quite close to me so they could open their door into mine when they leave.* She decided not to repark her car elsewhere. Guess what happened when she returned back to her car? Yes, that's right, she found a big dent on her car door, just as her intuition had been telling her!

When you develop and enhance your intuition, it gives you the ability to provide a much warmer, safer and more secure environment for your family, friends, clients, colleagues and wider community. You might notice that people start communicating more openly with you, sharing what's happening in their world because you have a sense that something is up and they need to talk about it. This increases rapport and builds trust within your relationships. People will feel like you understand them, that you just "get it" or they get the impression that perhaps you already know (or have an inkling) about what they wish to talk to you about.

Your intuition can give you signals to check in on people to make sure that they are OK. You might get that feeling that something isn't quite right. Have you ever thought of a family member or a friend, given them a call to check-in and discovered that they weren't well or needed assistance?

Intuition coupled with empathy allows you to come from a place of care, kindness and assistance. You can help boost the trust, communication and rapport that you have in both a personal and professional sense. Intuition when acted upon can foster and strengthen key relationships in your life. Imagine a world where people have increased intuition so that they can help themselves and each other. What a gift!

Getting Off Track

If you don't follow your intuition, it can take you off track from your vision and you certainly won't have crystal-clear clarity around who you are and what you do. You won't get to Make Your Mark as quickly as you might have if you *had* listened to your intuition. Trusting your gut can save you a lot of time. You can use it to learn to make decisions as to who you should work with, who you should hire, or who you should fire. The quicker you can tap into your intuition, and the quicker that you accept the messages, the better off you will be. Being open to your intuition allows you to become a vessel that downloads or channels information to help protect and guide you.

Do you get whispers of warnings or wonderment? Do you listen to them, or do you ignore them? Do you recall a time that you have gone against your intuition? If yes, what impact did that have for you and how did it affect you personally or professionally (or even both)?

Please believe that you really do know more than you give yourself credit for. It's time to back and trust yourself, let your intuition assist you to Make Your Mark.

MAKE YOUR MARK
Moment

Let me tell you about one of my experiences when I *didn't* follow my inner guru. I was having a meeting with a new client about assisting her with her business, and I felt the whisper that she wasn't going to be an ideal client. It was like a pebble stuck in my shoe, persistent and obvious; something I was constantly aware of, but easy to ignore. The client was great at paying in advance and I really wanted to help her bring her vision to life – what could go wrong?

In another session, my client mentioned that she didn't have people stick around too long in her life, that they just became a disappointment. It felt like a rock was being thrown at me this time – I literally heard a voice in my head say, "Jess, just deliver this one program and finalise your ties to this client." I took note of it, but still I ignored it. Eventually, the client became more and more needy, emailing and calling me at all hours of the day and night, demanding information and creation of materials immediately no matter what boundaries I was trying to establish with her. I started to get incredibly anxious when checking my emails or answering the phone, always thinking, *What's next?* I felt as though my work with other clients was starting to suffer as I wasn't sure how I could accommodate their needs with the limited time I had left over. I was also losing precious time with my family and found it difficult to "switch off". If only I had listened to my intuition early on, I would not have found myself in this unpleasant situation. Lesson learnt and well and truly noted ... Take note of those whispers and red flags, for if you don't, they can become a massive boulder that wipe you out completely. I had felt the pebble, and then the rock, yet I didn't take note until the boulder hit me.

Make Your Markercise

Intuition INDICATOR

Jessica Ritchie ©

Where do you rank on the Intuition Indicator? Take this quick quiz to find out! For each of the following questions, circle the answer that feels most correct for you. (Please note that this is not an in-depth quiz, but simply an indication of whether you might need to pay more attention to your intuition to assist you to Make Your Mark.)

1. Do you ever get a gut feeling, a hunch, a sixth sense, or a voice within?

    Yes, I always get those feelings. (5)

    I often get those feelings. (4)

    Sometimes I get those feelings. (3)

    Rarely do I get those feelings. (2)

    I never get those feelings. (1)

2. Have you ever had a time that you felt like your response to a certain person or situation was a "no", yet you went ahead and did it anyway?

   Yes, always. (5)

   Often. (4)

   Sometimes. (3)

   Rarely. (2)

   No, never. (1)

3. How do you feel when you listen to your intuition, and you follow the guidance?

   I feel empowered and confident. (5)

   It reiterates that I should trust it more. (4)

   Uncertain if I really did make the best decision. (3)

   I really stress myself out going back and forth. (2)

   I don't listen to my intuition at all. (1)

4. How often do you go against your intuition?

   I'm not aware of feeling any intuition at all. (1)

   I always go against my intuition. (2)

   More often than not I go against my intuition. (3)

   I listen to my intuition and most times I listen. (4)

   I never go against what my intuition is telling me. (5)

5. How might having increased intuition assist you?

   Increased conviction and confidence in myself. (5)

   Much quicker decision-making. (4)

   I'll feel better knowing that I won't second guess myself as much. (3)

   I'm not sure if I am confident in listening to my intuition yet but I will try. (2)

   It won't assist me at all. (1)

Take a look at each question and assess which number you have circled most frequently.

If you've circled mainly 1s: Your intuition is close to non-existent. It is up to you to decide if you wish to pursue learning more about it and allowing yourself to listen to your intuition to aid and guide you on your journey. Without, you may find life harder than what others experience.

If you've circled mainly 2s: On the rare occasion you will listen to your intuition but more often than not, you go against it. Slowly start to quieten the noise and you'll be surprised at your inner voice coming through.

If you've circled mainly 3s: You are open to trying to hone your intuition and be guided by the hunches that you get. Be curious about it and give it a go to strengthen your abilities.

If you've circled mainly 4s: You often use your intuition yet you still go against it from time to time which annoys you because you know that you should know better! You've seen and felt the benefits of listening to your intuition. Be mindful and confident in your abilities!

If you've circled mainly 5s: You are highly intuitive and in touch with your inner guidance system that is allowing you to make decisions confidently, quickly and with ease. You know what you need to do to tap into your intuition and it has become one of your superpowers.

MAKE YOUR MARK
Moment

I remember years ago, I went to a Women in Business Christmas party. I was running late, and I'd missed seeing the raffle table as I walked in to hurriedly take my seat. After the meal was served, I got this feeling that I needed to go and view the raffle prizes. The major prize was a VIP ticket to a Women in Leadership conference. I'd always wanted to go to this particular conference, however at that time I was still in the startup phase of my business and funds were limited. I just knew that I had to buy a raffle ticket! I could feel in my bones that I was meant to attend this conference. I happened to have just one five dollar note on me – the exact cost of one ticket to enter the raffle. And what do you know? I was the lucky winner of the raffle and took home the grand prize of VIP ticket to the Women in Leadership event. When I attend that prized event, it made me realise that I too could one day be a speaker and presenter at these types of events. I had held this belief that perhaps I wasn't good enough or that you had to be a rock star to do it, but following my intuition gave me the opportunity to see that this wasn't true; that I could do it. It was the fuel I needed to rocket launch my business even further.

Developing Your Intuition

You can make developing your intuition into a fun game. Be curious and creative about discovering and harnessing your intuitive abilities.

Write down when you feel or hear a sign, whether it's a whisper of warning or a whisper of wonder. I bet you will be saying to yourself in no time, "Hah, well, there you go, I was right; I should've listened and done what my gut said to do!"

It's important to listen to your gut. When you feel those hunches, or you feel sick to your stomach, break a sweat, or stop breathing properly, these are all signs that something might not be quite right, that you need to slow down and take notice of what might be happening.

Dreams can also provide us with guidance of what we should or shouldn't be doing, what we might be worried about or what is taking up our energy – try keeping a journal by your bed to record any lucid dreams and see if there is a pattern or message within them that might be useful for you.

Meditation is a fantastic tool that you can use to enhance and elevate your intuition as well. Meditation gives you the opportunity to be mindful, still and, preferably, silent. Start meditating for just three minutes per day to see what comes through, often you will get an idea or the answer to something you've been searching for.

I've been lucky enough to always have strong intuition. Was I born with it? I can't be certain of that, but what I know for sure is that I've learnt how to strengthen and harness it. Just because you might not feel overly intuitive doesn't mean that you aren't. It's like a muscle that needs to be exercised to increase its strength! Everyone can access their inner guru.

Here is how I tap into my inner guru and unlock my intuition:

1. Learn to tune into silence. Take time on a regular basis to sit alone in a quiet space, away from anyone or anything that requires your attention (including your mobile phone). Solitude and silence allow you to hear and feel your inner voice more easily. Practice this regularly so it becomes a ritual. Start to tune into silence and your inner voice when you're doing simple things like going for a walk or hanging the washing on the line. This will make it easier to tap into your intuition in more complex situations.

2. Pay attention to what you enjoy doing and when you feel in "flow". Flow is when you feel like you can do tasks and make decisions with ease. Everything feels relatively straightforward and flowing. When you increase your level of joy, so too do you increase your intuitive abilities.

3. If you're given a choice to do something, take note of how that makes you feel, of what your inner voice says to you. Make a mental note of this before saying what you THINK you have to do. Often, it's that voice

or feeling that tells you what is right or wrong before you say anything.

4. Practice mindfulness. Allow yourself the time to be connected to yourself, nature, and the world around you. Fresh air and sunshine are a wonderful way to ground yourself. Take off your shoes and walk barefoot on the ground, content with nothing more than being aware of your breath and watching the rustling of the leaves and the clouds in the sky.

5. Learn to pay attention to the signs and feelings that you receive as quickly as possible. Write them down if you have to. Write down your dreams too, as often our subconscious is wanting us to know something. You don't need to try and make sense of everything, just be led with what feels right.

> *"A woman knows by intuition or instinct what is best for herself."*
> — MARILYN MONROE

The more that you listen to your inner guru, the more you will feel empowered and confident in your decision-making. You can feel assured that you're being guided on your path for your best and highest good. It really is a superpower that you are blessed with, and it is up to **you** to tap into it and use it for all its worth.

Make Your Markercise

Intuition Reflection:

1. Write down a time, situation, or event when you have used or followed your intuition and had a successful outcome.
2. Write down a time, situation or event that you didn't use or follow your intuition. What was the outcome? Why didn't you follow you intuition in this case?
3. What strategies might you try to help tap into and develop your intuition?

1. _____

2. _____

3. _____

4. _____

5. _____

Intuition – Finding Your Inner Guru

STEP 11

Integrity – Even When Eyes Can't See

"Choosing courage over comfort; choosing what is right over what is fun, fast, or easy; and choosing to practice our values rather simply professing them."

— BRENÉ BROWN

There are a lot of "buzzwords" that are thrown about in the world. Buzzwords are jargon words or phrases that are popular at certain moments in time. Some words which have been popular in the last few years include "courageous leadership", "pivot", "authenticity". There's no doubt that these are all important concepts and most certainly assist you to Make Your Mark. One of the words, authenticity, is one of my core values. However, there's another word that ends in *y* that works alongside authenticity quite nicely which I think gets overlooked. It's sometimes too freely assumed and needs to be placed smack bang into the spotlight. I am talking about **integrity**. Integrity is imperative at all times to Make Your Mark.

Integrity is what you do and how you act even when NO ONE is watching. It is when you choose thoughts and actions based on your values rather than on personal gain or convenience.

The Traits of Integrity

When you have integrity, it means that you are living true to your values. You are being honest with yourself and all those with whom you're in contact with. It means:

- Keeping your word, and doing what you say that you're going to do. You "walk the walk" and "talk the talk"; you're not "all talk and no show".

- Being dependable and following through with your commitments to yourself and others.

- ✖ Being thoughtful of others.

- ✖ Accountability and owning up if you've made a mistake or about your shortcomings.

- ✖ Being reliable and trustworthy, and upholding confidentiality.

- ✖ Communicating openly and honestly.

- ✖ Being hardworking and committed at all times.

Each of the above traits are independent of each other, but integrity is the thread that holds them together.

Integrity is an **extremely** valuable trait and is something that almost everyone searches for and desires in others. When you live with integrity, you will find that you become people's confidant, mentor, teacher, carer and leader. Integrity is vital in all positions, but especially those that require trust and are an honour.

I had an experience where a new potential client reached out to me to have a coffee. Sylvia (not her real name) wanted to discuss which tier of my program she should purchase for her business. Aware that this new potential client had recently had major surgery, I took the process extra slowly, going through each level of the program and what it entailed. Sylvia decided she wanted to go "the full deal" and "go for gold." Having taken the time to get to know Sylvia and her business, I knew that she didn't need the Gold Program. Silver was what she needed but given that she was in a delicate place health-wise, and I could see just our meeting was taking up precious energy, I suggested that she start with the Bronze Program to take it a bit slower and that she could always upgrade to Silver at a later date.

I walked away from the meeting not knowing whether I'd be engaged to help Sylvia or not but a few days later she got back to me and said, "Thank you so much for your honesty. With my recent hospital stay, funds are tight and you're right, I don't need the full program." Someone with less integrity might have seen this as an opportunity to get as much money from Sylvia as possible, no matter what, but it has always been important to me that I show integrity in my brand, my values, while creating trust and connection with people. Treating Sylvia with integrity has had many benefits: she has remained a loyal and consistent client of mine ever since, and she has also recommended me to some of her key clients because of her experience with me.

From the other perspective, I once experienced a lovely display of integrity when my washing machine broke down one day. Kelvyn from Care Technical Solutions, a washing machine repairman with forty-five years' experience, displayed his integrity and his values of care immediately. He identified the part that may have been the issue (it was either that part or the circuit board, he said), and ordered it. When the part arrived and he came to fix the machine a few days later, he discovered that it was actually the circuit board of the washing machine that wasn't working, and not the part that he had ordered. Kelvyn didn't charge me for the part that he ordered, but said he was going to keep it on hand so that he would know immediately for other clients if they encountered the same problem. Kelvyn said, "Please don't replace the circuit board, you really are better off just getting a new washing machine." A new board would cost over six hundred dollars, including labour. Kelvyn only charged me his base rate yet delivered an abundance of service filled with care. If Kelvyn didn't have integrity, he could've charged me for the part, for a new circuit board, and plenty of labour and call-out fees, and I would have been none the wiser. In turn, I left Kelvyn a five-star review and have become a raving fan of his business. Whenever I hear someone needing washing machine repairs, Kelvyn from Care Technical Solutions is your man! Integrity might mean less immediate profit, but will pay dividends over time.

When Integrity Is Lost

A person who *lacks* integrity will make decisions based on how it will make them look or how they can benefit from a situation, rather than how it will benefit others.[23]

With a lack of integrity, your reputation can come crashing down quicker than a house of cards.

There is a saying that I hear repeated far too often: "Fake it until you make it." Perhaps it's the misalignment with one of my values of authenticity, but I really detest it. I feel it

---

23 Quy, LaRae, "This is the Best Way to Detect Lack of Integrity in Others," *The Ladders*, May 31, 2019, https://www.theladders.com/career-advice/the-best-way-to-detect-lack-of-integrity-in-others.

lacks integrity, and gives people permission to pretend and give off an impression that they are more than they truly are. I was at a business workshop a few years ago where the person holding the event proudly declared that they had read one book on marketing and that it sounded like a fun thing to do, so the next day they created a business specialising in marketing. I admired their confidence and self-belief, but what I found astounding was that they marketed themselves as an expert. On average, it takes ten years of honing a skillset to be deemed an expert in something. To me, reading one book didn't justify them having that title, and it wasn't fair to their customers who were being led to believe that they had more experience than they actually did. Unsurprisingly, their business didn't last long as people quickly realised that promised results weren't being achieved. If that person had been honest about their skillset and who they could specifically assist, then they would have been showing integrity.

This incident showcased to me how important it was for people to take the time to discover their identity and have a vision of what they want to do, but also the importance of putting in the time and effort to work out what they need to do to get there (such as training, education, building support networks, coaching, and always integrity through showcasing transparency of ability and results).

This behaviour is common in a lot of industries. The "fake it until you make it" mentality reminds me of "shake and pour" pancakes. You know those plastic containers that you purchase off the supermarket shelf containing pre-mixed pancake ingredients so you don't need to make them from scratch? You just add water, shake, and pour the mixture into a hot pan. It's a quick method, but they don't taste or look anywhere near as good as proper pancakes. And that might be fine if you're happy to exchange quality for speed, but there would be a problem if you use this quick method and tell people that you're making your pancakes from scratch. The person eating your pancakes will be disappointed if they discover that you've promised something you haven't delivered. They might be disappointed in the quality of what you've given to them, but they also might not notice at all. Regardless of whether they notice or not, where does this choice leave your integrity?

I'm not saying that "faking it until you make it" isn't sometimes a useful strategy. I believe that you can do mind hacks to create confidence within yourself when doing things for the first time and while you're still learning. I am a big fan of this. But I am also a big fan of honesty. This is where integrity comes in. If you're charging someone money or you are going to be spending a lot of time with them, be honest about your skillset and your objectives. We all have to start somewhere. If you're still learning or delivering a new service, be upfront and honest with your customer or client. It takes the pressure off you, and your clients and customers will trust you all the more for it.

It is your honour and duty to support people, not to benefit yourself.

> *"The safest road to hell is the gradual one – the gentle slope, soft underfoot, without sudden turnings, without milestones, without signposts."*
> — C. S. LEWIS

Keeping Integrity at the Forefront of Everything You Do

Integrity highlights the importance of clarity: of knowing who you are and having a strong sense of self, self-worth, and vision; of removing your fears and limiting beliefs; of tapping into your intuition; and holding your values dear by practicing them. It sometimes means making hard choices and doing what is right, over doing what is immediately profitable or personally beneficial. When you've got clarity and you've harnessed the aforementioned aspects of yourself, integrity becomes part of who you are in everything that you do.

We are in uncertain times – facing climate change, the rising cost of living, the ongoing global pandemic – which means that there is a lot of pressure on people's health, wellbeing, finances, home and job security. In uncertain times, we might be tempted to compromise our integrity in some parts of our lives to ensure security in other parts – for instance, upselling a more expensive program to a trusting but naive client for the financial security of your family. Integrity is easier when things are going smoothly, but as Judy Olian, dean of the Anderson School of Management at UCLA, advises, even when "there aren't clear rules and guidelines of dos and don'ts ... if it doesn't feel right, don't do it. Don't use the excuse of *everyone else is doing it.*"[24]

It doesn't matter what we might experience, integrity in your business, career and life shines through. It can provide us a lifeline in an unsettling, and unknown world. Remember: integrity – even when eyes can't see.

---

24 Eve Ash, "The Magnificent Seven Aspects of Integrity," *Smart Company*, August 24, 2015, https://www.smartcompany.com.au/people-human-resources/seven-components-that-make-up-integrity/

MAKE YOUR MARK
Moment

When I lost my home and everything inside it in the 2011 Queensland floods, an insurance assessor came out within a few days. By the time she got there, I'd had dozens of people, the volunteers who became known as the "Mud Army", come through to help clean up what they could, and get rid of what they couldn't – ripping up the destroyed carpets, pulling out damaged cupboards, etc. The assessor told me with tears in her eyes that my insurance company had told her not to approve any flood-related claims. She said the only way I could get a payout from my insurance was to make a claim against the Mud Army, proving that they had been "negligent" in the removing or throwing out of goods.

She also told me that she was going to resign the next day. She said she wouldn't be able to live with herself if she continued to work for that company, knowing that people had paid for insurance in good faith, yet they weren't going to be approved. I also wouldn't have been able to live with myself if I made a claim against the Mud Army when it was because of them I got through one of my toughest times. It was one of those bittersweet moments, each of us doing the right thing despite knowing that the wrong thing would have financial benefits – me through an insurance payout and her through a continued salary.

I am grateful to the accessor for her honesty and integrity. Her bold stand encouraged me to hold true to my integrity in that situation. It put a fire in my belly to later take a case against my insurance company to the ombudsman at the Australian Financial Complaints Authority, where I thankfully won and was paid out my rightful insurance claim.

STEP 12

Congruence Can Influence

> "There are certain things that are fundamental to human fulfillment. The essence of these needs is captured in the phrase 'to live, to love, to learn, to leave a legacy.' The need to leave a legacy is our spiritual need to have a sense of meaning, purpose, personal congruence, and contribution."
>
> — STEPHEN COVEY

Bringing It All Together

You have now got a firm understanding of what it takes to Make Your Mark, creating a solid foundation for you to understand and know:

- ✘ Your **sense of self** – truly owning your identity and the many facets that make you incredibly and irreplaceably YOU.

- ✘ Your **self-worth** – understanding the importance of owning your worth and to stop underestimating the value that you bring in everything that you do. If you don't value yourself, no one else will!

- ✘ Your **vision** – knowing where you are going with passion and purpose, giving yourself permission to dream by having goals, and harnessing your energy to live the life you deserve.

- ✘ Your **unique gifts** – allowing you to identify what your strengths are. You become aware of the "secret sauce" that you bring to life's table.

- ✘ Your **fears** – shining the spotlight on the darkness of your fears so that you can move forward feeling "light" and being the light for others. Removing the shackles of fear that hold you back from being your best self and living the life you imagine.

- ✖ Your **limiting beliefs** – understanding and releasing the stories that you tell yourself that aren't serving you for your best and highest good.

- ✖ **Imposter syndrome** – becoming the composer of your life so that the imposter that visits doesn't take up home within your heart and soul. Having the confidence to call out the thoughts that creep in, and step into your power.

- ✖ **Comparisonitis** – don't even dare to compare as you will lose your joy, momentum, and your passion. There is no other you in this universe – that is your power so don't give it away to someone else who isn't you!

- ✖ Your **values** – knowing your values and core values brings clarity around who you are and everything that you stand for. These are the guiding lights behind your thoughts and actions and keeping in alignment.

- ✖ Your **intuition** – listening to your inner guru, that compass that guides you. Your intuition provides whispers of warning or whispers of wonder so you can feel when you are aligned.

- ✖ Your **integrity** – there is no longer a gap between your intent and your behaviour. You know your values and you live them whether people are watching or not, or whether it benefits you or not.

The final piece of your foundation, and the one that really solidifies it and brings it all together is to be in **congruence**. Congruence is generally defined as "agreement or harmony; compatibility".[25] I define congruence as when your head and your heart align internally with your thoughts, and externally with your actions. It is when you and your ideal self are intertwined and working harmoniously together on your journey to becoming your best self. Are you already able to start feeling the sense of relief, empowerment and flow that comes with congruence?

I love this quote about being congruent from leadership expert and author Robin Sharma: "It's about knowing who you are, what you stand for, and then having the courage to be yourself – in every situation rather than only when it's convenient. It's about being real, consistent and congruent so who you are on the inside is reflected by the way you perform on the outside."[26]

The benefits of being in congruence are many, and include:

- More confidence within yourself and in your interactions with others.

- An increase in momentum and productivity in all that you do as you're driven towards your goals.

---

25 *Lexico,* s.v. "Congruence," accessed November 3, 2021, https://www.lexico.com/definition/congruence.

26 Robin Sharma, *The Leader Who Had No Title: A Modern Fable on Real Success in Business and in Life* (New York: Free Press, 2010), 75.

- A higher level of energy, because you're remaining true to who you are. Decision fatigue is reduced as you live in alignment.

- Increased feelings of peace, joy and living in the moment. You are living with intention, with less anxiety about the future and less dwelling in the past.

- Life seems to unfold with more grace and ease, instead of feeling like it is full of friction and conflict.

- You are trusted and held in high stead within yourself and by others.

When You Aren't Congruent

The opposite of congruence is conflict. If you are not congruent with who you are and what you're doing, you're in conflict. You are out of alignment, and you can feel uncertain, uncomfortable, annoyed, incompatible and in disagreement with yourself and others. Not being congruent is what holds you back from making your mark.

The internal conflict that you can feel when you are not congruent can be the hesitation and uncertainty caused by not knowing who you are, and not having a strong sense of self. It can be caused by the negative self-talk we engage in and we allow ourselves to listen to. It can be the low self-worth and value that we have and the limiting beliefs that we allow to hold us back. It can also be imposter syndrome that rears its head to try and hold us back, or comparisonitis that sets in when we dare to compare. Conflict occurs when you don't know your values and are not living by your values. It is these conflicts that take you off course and prevent you from making your mark.

Having a firm understanding of what it takes to Make Your Mark and building the foundation to do that reduces the conflict you may feel and find at times within yourself.

> *"When there is no enemy within, the enemies outside cannot hurt you."*
> — AFRICAN PROVERB

When you are in congruence, there is another additional benefit. It means that you can be a beacon of influence. Congruence provides you with the ability to influence because it builds **trust**. We trust those who have integrity. We are attracted to those who know who they are and where they are going; those who do what they say they are going to do, and consistently live and breathe their values.

Being in congruence allows you to influence yourself first and foremost, ensuring that you remain internally aligned. When you are internally aligned then you will naturally influence others to do the same: to live congruently with their head and heart, to be internally aligned so that the external is like a mirror reflecting their internal state. When you use your congruence to influence, it helps others to make THEIR mark too.

When you are congruent, the lens you look through is not one of competition, but one of potential for collaboration. You are CONFIDENT. You don't spend your energy worried about what your competitors or other people are doing. If you've set a solid foundation with the key fundamentals, you will Make Your Mark – through consistency with congruency.

I witnessed a display of congruence recently when my friend was launching a business and only a few streets away, she discovered, was another business with a very similar concept. When the other owner found out there would be business like hers close by, she came by my friend's workplace to see for herself. Her shoulders were so tight and tense that they almost reached her ears, her eyes were wide in horror, and you could sense that her heart was sinking. My friend said, "Oh no, please don't despair, this is truly wonderful news! We can help each other, leverage each other and support each other." My friend has such a strong sense of self with an unshakeable core value of service and assistance to others, that she didn't see the other business as a threat at all! The other woman looked relieved, her tension visibly dissipating. "Yes, you're so right!" she excitedly said. The women exchanged information that the other was having difficulty in finding, and shared stories of triumphs and challenges that they were both experiencing. To me, this was a wonderful example of how we can work in business, career and in life when we are living congruently. It means the reduction of stress, anxiety, and a scarcity mindset. It means a big, warm hello to more creativity, confidence, compassion and connection through congruence. I believe the world has taught us in the wake of COVID-19 that there is no such thing as competitors, there are only potential collaborators.

My story of congruence was when I connected and integrated my other passions such as being a reiki master, a neuro-linguistic programming practitioner and a life coach into my business model. Once I did that, and I was helping people through these modalities as well as branding and marketing, I felt like I could breathe! I now LOVED what I did. I woke up every day feeling light, relaxed, on point. It felt right within my bones, my heart, to the depth of my soul. This was it. This was me. This is what I am meant to do. I felt like I had arrived back home to myself. That I had had a missing puzzle piece that was now firmly in place. I could *see* the big picture; I *was* the big picture. I was now congruent in all that I did. I was making my mark for myself, and for others.

MAKE YOUR MARK
Moment

I witnessed what I think is a wonderful example of living in congruence at the Tokyo 2020 Olympics by Australian athlete Cedric Dubler. He was competing in the decathlon, a gruelling ten-event athletic competition, with his friend and teammate Ashley Moloney. On entering the final event, a fifteen hundred metre run, Dubler was out of contention for a medal, but Moloney was well positioned and just needed to do well in this final event to secure a medal. Noticing Moloney struggling during the run, Dubler sacrificed his own time in that individual event, running with Moloney, setting the pace and yelling encouraging words to boost his energy. This support helped Moloney cross the finish line with a personal best time for the race, and claim bronze in the decathlon event. Despite not being able to get a medal himself, Dubler showed that he was a cheerleader and support for his friend. As a two-time Olympic competitor, Cedric knew the time, effort, sacrifice, commitment, courage, and resilience that it takes to reach that elite level. He didn't let his disappointment at going home without a medal stop him from helping his mate get one. Ashley received the bronze medal, but the look on Cedric's face was so joyful, it was like he had also won. They are both winners in different ways: Ashley for becoming an Australia's first Olympic decathlon medallist, and Cedric for epitomising living your values. It makes me think of the quote, "We rise by lifting others." It was a wonderful display of someone living in congruence with their vision, their passion, their worth, their strong sense of self, their values and integrity to get a mate over the line as a winner. Thanks, Cedric, for paving the way and showing that congruence can influence not only yourself, but others to make their mark.

Make Your Markercise

The Make Your Mark Mastery Identifier:

Once you have completed the Markercises within each step, fill out the Mastery Identifier to get a tangible view of where you're performing well and where you may need to invest some more time to Make Your Mark. You may like to concentrate on one step each month to ensure you establish a routine and harness that skill over a twelve-month period. It is completely up to you to decide whether you want to crawl, walk or run!

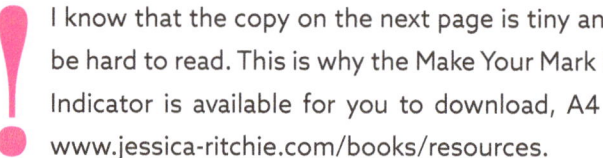

I know that the copy on the next page is tiny and might be hard to read. This is why the Make Your Mark Mastery Indicator is available for you to download, A4 size, at www.jessica-ritchie.com/books/resources.

"MAKE YOUR MARK"
Mastery Identifier©

Now that you have read Make Your Mark if you haven't done so already, take the time to complete each of the exercises or prompts at the end of each chapter.

MAKE YOUR MARK is all about laying a strong foundation so that you have clarity and a vision to be your best self with confidence. To step into your personal power. Reflect on where you are currently positioned with the below statements. Place a mark on the scale beside each statement as to where you feel you are at. Each statement reflects a chapter of Make Your Mark. At the bottom of the sheet, tally the numbers that you have to reflect your final Make Your Mark score. This will provide you with insight into where your strengths lie and which areas you may need to boost to ensure a solid foundation to go forth and Make Your Mark™!

Not at all/ Never	2	3	4	Somewhat/ Often	6	7	8	9	Very/ Yes

SENSE OF SELF - IDENTITY
I have a strong sense of self - I understand all the facets that I encompass that form my identity and I feel balanced.

SELF WORTH
I value myself, my time and feel secure in asking for what I believe I deserve. I am well paid.

VISION
I know what my purpose is and what it is that I need to do to achieve my Vision and stay on track. I am excited about the future.

UNIQUE GIFTS
My unique gifts are known by those in my industry, and I know how my gifts set me a part from others.

FEAR
I move throughout life with flow, grace and ease without fear and try new things, despite a sense of unease.

LIMITING BELIEFS
I am aware of thoughts and beliefs that are not for my best and highest good and can re-frame the negative beliefs into assets that support my goals.

IMPOSTER SYNDROME
I am aware of the internal conversations that can derail my success and only listen to positive self-talk.

COMPARISONITIS
I stick to my own lane and don't mind what others are doing. I keep my energy and focus to my vision and don't allow myself to get caught up in the highlight reels of others.

VALUES
I know my values and my core values so that I can make quick decisions that align to my vision and stay true to me at all times.

INTUITION
I use my intuition as an internal compass to guide me to making the best decisions based on my gut instinct. When I do this, I am usually right with my decisions.

INTEGRITY
At all times I am living my values in my thoughts and my actions. I do what I say and I say what I do, even it can be difficult, I will do the right thing.

CONGRUENCE
My values, intuition and integrity provide me with a robust foundation to be my best, authentic self where I am living in alignment.

ADD UP EACH COLUMN. Total of 1-5s column: ___ Total of 6-10s columns: ___.
Transfer your numbers for each over to the following table and mark your progress from the bottom up as aim to even the levels of each over a 12-month period – focusing on improving one area per month. (Of course, you can fast track if you are a go-getter!) Focus on the lowest areas first. Your objective is to even up your overall position.

www.transformationalbrandlab.com

Congruence Can Influence

Twelve-Month Goal Setting Targets:

	1	2	3	4	5	6	7	8	9	10	11	12
SENSE OF SELF – IDENTITY I have a strong sense of self - I understand all the facets that I encompass that form my identity and I feel balanced.												
SELF WORTH I value myself, my time and feel secure in asking for what I believe I deserve. I am well paid.												
VISION I know what my purpose is and what it is that I need to do to achieve my Vision and stay on track. I am excited about the future.												
UNIQUE GIFTS My unique gifts are known by those in my industry, and I know how my gifts set me a part from others.												
FEAR I move throughout life with flow, grace and ease without fear and try new things, despite a sense of unease.												
LIMITING BELIEFS I am aware of thoughts and beliefs that are not for my best and highest good and can re-frame the negative beliefs into assets that support my goals.												
IMPOSTER SYNDROME I am aware of the internal conversations that can derail my success and only listen to positive self-talk.												
COMPARISONITIS I stick to my own lane and don't mind what others are doing. I keep my energy and focus to my vision and don't allow myself to get caught up in the highlight reels of others.												
VALUES I know my values and my core values so that I can make quick decisions that align to my vision and stay true to me at all times.												
INTUITION I use my intuition as an internal compass to guide me to making the best decisions based on my gut instinct. When I do this, I am usually right with my decisions.												
INTEGRITY At all times I am living my values in my thoughts and my actions. I do what I say and I say what I do, even it can be difficult. I will do the right thing.												
CONGRUENCE My values, intuition and integrity provide me with a robust foundation to be my best, authentic self where I am living in alignment.												

12 MONTH GOAL SETTING TARGETS TO MAKE YOUR MARK™

Final Thoughts

Time is precious and I am immensely grateful to you for spending your time reading my book. I hope that I have given you even just one thing that you can implement in your life and make tangible magic with.

As I mentioned at the start of this book, the "Make Your Mark" concept came to me through both personal and professional experiences. Through those experiences, I discovered twelve key concepts and the potential that can be achieved through focusing on MARK – mindset, authenticity, resilience and kindness. You now have the tools to build a solid foundation of clarity and vision that's infused with your identity, self-worth, unique gifts, values, intuition, integrity and congruence. You have the ability to remove the limiting beliefs that have been holding you back, and you can kick comparisonitis and imposter syndrome to the curb! Grab your director's chair, harness the power of your Personal Power Anthem and Make Your Mark Mantras to march to the beat of your drum to pave (or blaze!) your own path. Be sure to keep revisiting this book and mapping out where you are on your journey by using the Make Your Mark Mastery Indicator (p. 214) and the Make Your Mark Scale (p. 3). It is my intention that you will go from being a "Striver" to being a "Thriver".

Life is a journey and we each have a map that unfolds for us each day. We can't know exactly what lies ahead, but we can look back and see what has been. Each mark that you make through your increased clarity will now be more visible on your map of life. When you look back (reflection is a great tool!), you will be able to see the strong, intentional marks you've made, and the smaller marks that are scattered in between. By focusing on the four elements of MARK and harnessing a positive mindset, authenticity, resilience and kindness combined with these twelve key steps, you have the ability to set intentional and bolder marks for your future. Place your mark on your map. X marks the spot to treasure, and that treasure is you and the gifts of your unique energy and essence that only you can provide to the world.

All marks have an impact on ourselves and others. It is now up to you step up, step out and Make Your Mark in the world.

The marks you make will create a ripple effect out into the world, ripples that will make it a better place. By shining your light brightly, you will inspire and empower others. What a legacy you can begin to create – in your business, career, and your life – through having a strong foundation and discovering clarity and vision to become your best self.

Keep in touch at jessica@jessica-ritchie.com; I'd love to hear how you're going on your transformational journey.

It's time for you to Make Your Mark!

With grit and (a dash of) grace,

Jess

Jessica Wants to Hear from You!

I'm grateful for the time that you've taken to read my book. The next steps so that I can continue to help you on your journey are:

Free goodies

Remember to collect your FREE swag of goodies that I have created to help supercharge your journey to becoming a Make Your Mark Maestro! To download your **free gifts**, go to https://jessica-ritchie.com/books/resources.

Be the first …

Be the first to know the latest news and learn new techniques to enrich your life, career, and business by subscribing to Jessica's newsletter, at www.transformationalbrandlab.com.

Want to be featured?

Have you applied any of the techniques within this book and want to share your experience with Jessica and the "Your Mark" community? Email your story to hello@transformationalbrandlab.com and you may be featured in the "Mark Makers" section of Jessica's newsletter.

Work with Jessica

Jessica is available to share the Make Your Mark techniques with you and your audience, association, or employees. Work with Jessica one-on-one, invite her to host a half- or full-day workshop, or register for one of her public workshops. Discover for yourself why Jessica is a multi-award-winning brand expert and receives rave reviews for her presentations that leave audiences thinking, laughing, empowered and inspired to take action in their business, career and in life. Visit www.jessica-ritchie.com and www.transformationalbrandlab.com for more information, or email jessica@transformationalbrandlab.com.

Acknowledgements

It has taken me five years to bring this book to life. When I finally decided to be diligent with my writing, I pulled out the folder I kept, which contained hundreds of scrap pieces of paper and napkins scrawled with thoughts, insights and ideas ranging from just one word to thousands. This book was born through many midnight musings and hundreds of candid client conversations. I continue to use the ideas in this book daily as my own guide to make my own mark and shine bright in the world. It is my hope that they become a useful guide for you, too.

I could not have written this book without the support, love and encouragement of so many people and for that I am grateful.

To my husband, Sam. Thank you from the bottom of my heart for your unwavering support and belief in me. For the cups of tea that you make me while I work (some left stone cold if I am on a roll!), and for putting up with my restless nights' sleep when I get up and down countless times to write down or work on my ideas. Thank you for allowing me to share some of our stories that have formed our journey and parts of this book. I love you.

To my sons, Max and Billy. Thank you for being my greatest teachers, and the most valuable gifts I have and will ever receive in my life. You guys make me a better person every day and I love the lens through which you both view life. I am one proud mum.

Special thanks to my Mum and Dad – for your endless love, support, and belief in me, always. You are always there for me no matter what. Thank you just doesn't seem enough.

To Rhonda and Bryan – every day I am grateful to have scored the most helpful, generous and supportive in-laws in the world.

To my Grandma Bernice – you had a dream of writing your own book and I hope in some small way that this book brings you joy. You are always on my shoulder.

To my Nana Jess and Nanu Ned, thank you for the perfect balance of love and practicality that you've continually shown me.

To my brothers, Nathan and Justin; sisters-in-law, Samantha and Jade; and my nieces, Maddison and Charlotte – thank you for your love, for having my back, and for your endless support.

Thank you to my beta readers, Larissa Simonsen, Samantha Grima, and Kathy Rees, and to my reviewers. Thank you for being the first people to lay eyes on my book and provide me constructive feedback and support. Larissa, you're a gem who has encouraged me no end to chase my dreams and to sparkle and shine.

To Dixie, Ann, Anne-Marie, Daniela, Michelle and the team at Indie Experts – what a wonderful journey this has been. Thank you for assisting me to finally bring this book to life!

To Lindsey Nolan and Emma Mactaggart – for your beautiful friendship, generosity and brains trust.

To my mentors past and present and to my high 5 crew and friends – you know who you are, and I am so grateful to be on this ride called life with you.

To my wonderful clients – without you, I would not be paving my path and leaving a legacy like I am now. It is an honour and joy the trust that you place in me to assist you in creating transformational brands and businesses through strategic marketing, branding and better "balance" through energy elevation.

And last but not least, thank YOU, the reader, for choosing to invest your valuable time into reading my book. It is my wish that you find some inspiration and encouragement to dive deep into rediscovering your best self and shining your light bright into the world.

About Jessica Ritchie

Jessica Ritchie is a multi-award-winning brand expert, consultant, speaker and business coach. Jessica creates transformational personal and business brands through strategic marketing and personal energy management.

Founder of the Transformational Brand Lab, Jessica works with high-performing, emerging leaders, entrepreneurs and business owners to create clarity, connect and communicate with confidence.

A certified marketing practitioner with over fifteen years' experience creating and working with some of Australia's leading and most recognised brands, Jessica is also a judge for several business awards.

Jessica is also a reiki master, neurolinguistic programming practitioner and certified life coach. These skills give her exceptional insight into the energy and essence of individuals and businesses, to help them amplify their uniqueness across their marketing and branding, and reach their full potential.

Jessica loves going on adventures near and far with her husband Sam, sons Max and Billy and her hyperactive Australian bulldog Missy.

www.jessica-ritchie.com

Coming Soon in the "Your Mark" Series

SPARK *Your Mark* – Connection to cultivate resilience and elevate your energy to sparkle in business, career and life.

IGNITE *Your Mark* – Communicate with confidence and amplify your visibility in business, career and life.

Now it's time to SPARK *YOUR* MARK

Spark that sense of liveliness or excitement. It's time to go to the next level on the "Your Mark" journey by striking a match to create a spark within through connection and elevating your energy.

In order to do this, we need that spark that allows us to be our best self. To step into our personal power.

*To be the sparkle,
be the trailblazer,
be the illuminator,
be the flame that burns bright.
To be the fire.*

Create that inner spark, nurture it, protect it, never let it burn out. The world needs you and your spark, to Spark Your Mark in your career and life.

A spark is defined as **"a small fiery particle thrown off from a fire, alight in ashes, or produced by striking together two hard surfaces such as stone or metal."**[27]

I've experienced a fiery particle from a fire that caused a spark and fuelled changes in my life beyond my imagination. I open up about these changes in this book. It's OK to turn up your spark and to turn it down (if required), but never, ever do you let it burn out or a worse, allow someone else to blow it out.

Why Is Your Spark Needed?

Have you ever heard anyone say, "I don't know, I can't quite put it into words, but they just have this *spark* about them?" It's attractive, it's powerful, it encourages, it inspires, and ultimately, it ignites others. How the heck do you get that spark, though? Well, that's what you will discover in this book.

In a highly competitive world, your spark can be the

---

27 *Lexico*, s.v. "Spark", accessed October 30, 2021, https://www.lexico.com/definition/spark.

difference between you being chosen for an opportunity, or turned down. Your spark is unique and sets you apart from others. It's important to allow it to shine through.

A spark allows people to have greater connection and confidence within themselves. A team or business full of people with sparks creates a more connected and cohesive team that has increased levels of creativity, engagement and productivity. If each person brings their spark to work, it can be the fuel to the fire of success for everyone, both personally and professionally.

One challenge to people's sparks is that they, women in particular, often play many roles simultaneously. This can lead to multiple role conflict, and can often leave us tired, and even burnt out. Change can throw us off kilter. Too busy to take time out, to reset and heal, we find ourselves like a hamster on a wheel, too scared to get off. This can create an identity crisis, a lack of sense of self. When we take away all of the roles: mother, partner, carer, sister, daughter, business owner, business partner, employee, volunteer, neighbour ... many people do not know who they are, at the very core of their essence. They've lost their spark.

Then there's the people in the world who will try and bring you down, to tear you down. They don't like to see your spark shining bright. These *spark snuffers* can even be those who are closest to us, such as family, friends, or colleagues – or even yourself.

> *"You wander from room to room hunting for the diamond necklace that is already around your neck."*
> — RUMI

Spark Your Mark focuses on twelve key steps to regenerate your spark, and to turn the heat up a few notches to ensure that it burns bright. Shine your light bright! Spark your mark for others, Spark Your Mark for YOU. Be the light. Shimmer. Shine.

Now that you can Make Your Mark, it is time to take it one step further to BE THE SPARK. Let's go Spark Your Mark.

Spark Your Mark, the second book in the inspiring "Your Mark" series by Jessica Ritchie, will be published in 2022. For updates on the release date of this book, please visit www.jessica-ritchie.com.

About Jana Stanfield, CSP

Multi-Platinum Songwriter
Professional Speaker
Founder, Together for Good Worldwide
Co-Founder, Together We Can Change the World
https://www.janastanfield.com

You've heard Jana's compositions on 20/20, *Entertainment Tonight*, *Oprah*, on radio stations, and sung by Reba McEntire and many others.

To widen her global understanding, Jana spent ten years traveling the world, speaking at international conferences and leading volun-tour trips with the motto: "The life you change may be your own." Jana truly embraces the concept of making your mark in the world.

Seeing young girls' disadvantages if they didn't have funds for education, she co-founded an international non-profit charity called Together We Can Change the World, which you can visit at www.twcctw.org.

Her latest humanitarian project is Together for Good Worldwide, at www.refugeefilmschool.com. Teaching refugee teens how to earn money for their families with video editing, Jana started the Refugee Film School as a pilot project: "Helping refugee teens build a bridge for their families ... from refugee to free digitally."

During the COVID-19 pandemic, Jana's lyrics were used in a national campaign in the USA: "We cannot do all the good that the world needs, but the world needs all the good that we can do."

www.ingramcontent.com/pod-product-compliance
Lightning Source LLC
Chambersburg PA
CBHW051541010526
44107CB00064B/2803